MANGA IN LIBRARIES

ALA Editions purchases fund advocacy, awareness, and accreditation programs for library professionals worldwide.

Jillian Rudes

MANGA
IN LIBRARIES

A Guide for Teen Librarians

ALA
Editions

CHICAGO | 2023

JILLIAN RUDES (she/her) is the school librarian at a grade 6–12 public school in New York City. She is the Japanese culture and manga librarian for the New York City Department of Education, as well as the founder of Manga in Libraries, a company which provides readers' advisory lists and hosts webinars, panels, and workshops. She received the American Association of School Librarians' (AASL) Collaborative School Library Award in 2020 and the American Library Association's (ALA) Scholastic Library Publishing Award in 2022. She was also deemed the "Manga Maven" by *Library Journal* and was selected as a *Library Journal* Mover & Shaker in 2022. Jillian has presented on manga at New York Comic Con, San Diego Comic Con, ALA's Annual Conference, the International Association of School Librarianship's Annual Conference, and more. You can find a ton of resources on her website at MangaInLibraries.com and can follow her on Twitter @JRlibrarian. You can also follow updates at #ReadManga.

© 2023 by Jillian Rudes

Extensive effort has gone into ensuring the reliability of the information in this book; however, the publisher makes no warranty, express or implied, with respect to the material contained herein.

ISBN: 978-0-8389-3861-4 (paper)

Library of Congress Cataloging-in-Publication Data
Names: Rudes, Jillian, 1981- author.
Title: Manga in libraries : a guide for teen librarians / Jillian Rudes.
Description: Chicago : ALA Editions, 2023. | Includes bibliographical references and index. | Summary: "This text provides an overview of manga in libraries for teen librarians. It covers how to build a manga collection, select age-appropriate manga for your readers, and host manga programming"— Provided by publisher.
Identifiers: LCCN 2022051913 | ISBN 9780838938614 (paperback)
Subjects: LCSH: Libraries—Special collections—Graphic novels. | Libraries—Special collections—Comic books, strips, etc. | Young adults' libraries—Collection development. | Graphic novels. | Young adults' libraries—Activity programs.
Classification: LCC Z692.G7 R83 2023 | DDC 025.2/77415—dc23/eng/20230106
LC record available at https://lccn.loc.gov/2022051913

Book design by Alejandra Diaz in the FreightText Pro and Bilo typefaces.

♾ This paper meets the requirements of ANSI/NISO Z39.48-1992 (Permanence of Paper).

Printed in the United States of America
27 26 25 24 23   5 4 3 2 1

CONTENTS

CONTENTS

ACKNOWLEDGMENTS

Thank you to all the experts who participated in interviews for this book: Erica Friedman, Laura Neuzeth, Victoria Rahbar, Renee Scott, Karina Quilantan-Garza, Tiffany Coulson, Deb Aoki, Sara Smith, and Robin Brenner.

Thank you to everyone who continues this journey with Manga in Libraries!

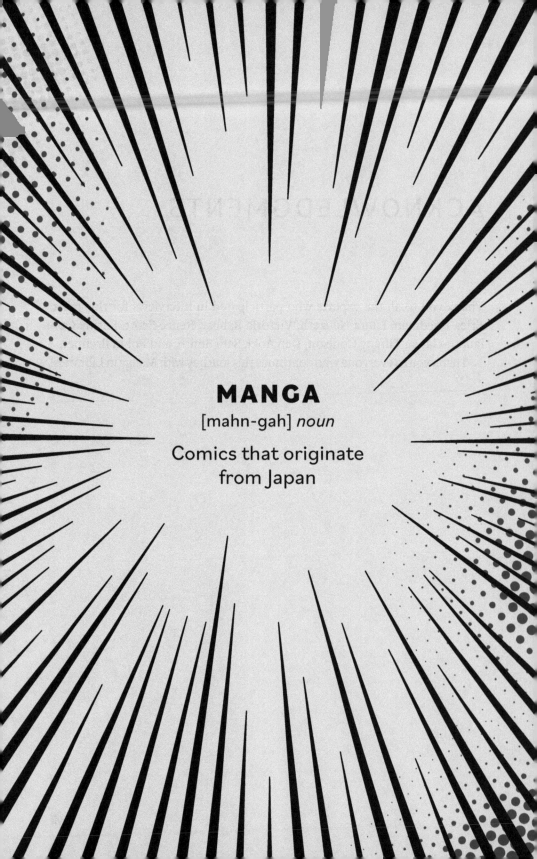

MANGA

[mahn-gah] *noun*

Comics that originate
from Japan

INTRODUCTION
Why Manga?

Readers should have access to manga in their libraries because of its emotional and epic storytelling, its unique and breathtaking artwork, its relatable and transformative stories about humanity, and the endless variety of genres, characters, conflicts, and plots found in its pages. Manga is by far the most-read medium in my library, and readers visit multiple times a day to borrow it from the collection. There is definitely no one type of reader; patrons of every age, gender, background, and reading level read manga. So, if readers want to read manga, your library should provide them with access to it.

MANGA EMPOWERS READERS

For many of us, visual storytelling is what makes manga so engaging. We are consumed daily with visual media: television, movies, video games, and social media. These are all examples of visual storytelling, visual media that we are engaged with. Visual media grabs our attention and connects to our emotions, and those emotions are what allow us to make connections to the content. Manga is just another example of the visual media that we consume as a society.

Many of us also read manga to escape the reality of our daily lives and to reduce stress. Runners say that they get addicted to running because their bodies begin to crave exercise. I think the same goes for reading, as our minds also crave exercise. I read every day, and the moment I open a book, my blood pressure drops, my shoulders relax, and my mind frees and expands itself as I get lost in a story. This is something that I tell educators and parents all the time, when they express their concern that a teen is reading "too much" manga. I remind them that we want teens to fall in love with the feeling of reading. Reading manga is pleasurable, safe, and freeing for readers.

I also think what engages many manga readers is that one can find a personal affinity for or a personal connection with a character. Manga usually focuses on the story of a main character, and the reader follows that character and lives through their experiences. Manga allows readers to be exposed to different perspectives, to the representation of diverse lived experiences, and to the conflicts and growth that will support their own personal development. I think this is particularly helpful for readers who are still trying to find their way in the world. It helps readers to understand themselves and their relationship to the world. Manga can also carry universal human truths and that may be why it is read all around the world.

Essentially, manga can empower readers. Through visual storytelling and character connections, manga can help build a reader's confidence and independence. Readers can develop their critical thinking skills and become responsible decision-makers. They can also make emotional connections that motivate them to persevere.

MANGA ENHANCES LITERACY

Reading manga can lead to a lifelong love of reading. Manga not only engages a community of readers, but it can also create new readers. Manga can increase reading engagement and boost the reading confidence of readers. Manga readers are among the most dedicated and voracious of all readers. They read more because there are multiple volumes in many manga series, and they read consistently because manga connects to their personal stories.

MANGA SUPPORTS A VARIETY OF LEARNING STYLES AND LITERACIES

Manga allows readers to build visual literacy skills, which includes understanding and interpreting the reading direction, frames, text bubbles, visual clues, and Japanese Visual Language. This language is the visual vocabulary and the visual representation of a character's emotions and thoughts. This visual information gives readers context clues so that they can decode and infer character motivation, conflict, and resolve.

Manga stories are complex and allow readers to engage in an analysis of literary devices such as plot, theme, symbolism, foreshadowing, conflict, and character development (through emotions, thoughts, words, and actions), which allows for a higher level of critical thinking.

Manga also helps readers develop verbal literacy and communication skills, especially since there is not an overwhelming amount of text on a page like prose. As such, readers can build their vocabulary and comprehension skills by pairing the visuals and the text to make inferences and interpret meaning.

Manga offers readers an opportunity to reflect on the storyline and characters, as well as the art style of the *mangaka* (manga artist). Readers can focus on the format and the style of manga, which includes panel (size and design), shading, tone, patterns, textures, imagery, and the relationship between the text and the art. Not only can readers enhance their art appreciation skills, but they also can enhance their art technique skills by engaging in lessons about the manga art style.

Age-appropriate manga can also be a support system for the social-emotional development of readers. Manga can often reflect the lives of readers and their lived personal experiences, which can help them find self-acceptance, as well as build empathy and interpersonal skills. Many titles focus on issues like friendships, dating, and sex, as well as bullying, anxiety, and overcoming obstacles.

Manga also provides readers with the opportunity to become culturally literate. Manga is often a lens into Japanese culture where readers can learn about school life, food and cooking, religion, history, fashion, holidays and celebrations, music, sports, and more.

*Excerpted from Jillian Rudes, "A School Librarian's Journey through Manga Collection Development," *Knowledge Quest* 50, no. 4 (2022): 37–38.

MANGA TRANSFORMS LIVES

Everything we want readers to learn and experience can happen through manga. It is our job as librarians to make sure that we continue to offer these opportunities for readers to not only read manga but also to reflect on what they have read, to share what they have read, and to celebrate what they have read.

MANGA 101

IN JAPAN, MANGA WAS INITIALLY CREATED TO entertain and provide literacy support to readers, but manga has since spread throughout the world, and there is now a widespread awareness of this global phenomenon. There is a lot to learn about building a manga collection, designing manga programming, and providing equitable manga services. To make the best decisions about developing a library culture that celebrates manga, it is essential that you have a foundational knowledge of this popular medium.

WHAT IS MANGA?

Manga (pronounced mahn-gah), which means "whimsical pictures," are comics created and published in Japan. The term *manga* originated in the nineteenth century but did not apply to manga as we know it until the twentieth century. The panels and text bubbles in manga are read from right-to-left in the Japanese style, in contrast to Western comics, which are read from left-to-right. Manga is published in black-and-white, although sometimes manga can include pages with color.

Manga is often published and sold in *tankobons* (individual volumes). These individual volumes include multiple chapters and are often one part of a series. These multiple chapters usually first appear in installments in weekly or monthly Japanese print or digital magazines. Manga series can have multiple *tankobons*, so make sure to consider the space available in your library and your budget before building a manga collection.

A BRIEF HISTORY OF JAPANESE VISUAL STORYTELLING

Japan has a long history of visual and narrative storytelling. Dating all the way back to the Nara period in Japan were *emakimono* (picture scrolls). *Emakimono*, created on long rolls of either rice paper or silk, were horizontal and often included calligraphy and illustrations to depict the sequence of everyday life events of the Japanese people. *Emakimono* were told in chronological order, and the scrolls were slowly unrolled as the story progressed. There was also *sumi-e* (ink-and-brush painting), which was brought to Japan by Zen Buddhist monks. *Sumi-e* was horizontal, monochrome, and consisted of simply lined ink-and-brush paintings that combined calligraphy, poetry, and nature. *Sumi-e* was used to capture the beauty and complexity of the natural world.

Advancements in visual storytelling led to *ukiyo-e* (woodblock prints) during the Edo period in Japan. *Ukiyo-e* depicted the interests of the people in Japan, which included samurai, geishas, kabuki actors, sumo wrestlers, and supernatural folktales. *Ukiyo-e* was created by carving a design into a woodblock, then inking and pressing the woodblock onto Japanese mulberry paper; colors were then added by hand. Woodblock printing led to the creation of *kusazoshi* (illustrated books). These books were about ten pages long and made up of folded and bound paper that depicted the events of everyday life in Japan. Dominated by illustrations, these books were color-coded by genres. There were *kibyoshi* books for adults, identified by a yellow cover; and there were *akahon* books for children, identified by a red cover. *Akahon* was a popular form of entertainment, but with the advent of the printing press, it would soon be replaced by *manga*.

There were also the performance arts, another type of visual storytelling in Japan. *Kabuki* theater (Japanese drama) included all sorts of audiovisual performances such as dancing, miming, and singing, as well as music on the *shamisen* (a three-stringed instrument). There were also elaborate costumes, wigs, and *kumadori* (stage makeup for kabuki actors). The *kumadori* allowed actors to visually express emotions on their face, with exaggerated lines around their mouth and eyes, and symbolic colors that represented human emotions. During the Great Depression, *kamishibai* (paper theater), also known as street theater, became a popular form of storytelling. *Kamishibaiya* (storytellers) would create hand-painted original art on storyboards and combine these illustrations with narrative storytelling. These small wooden stages for *kamishibai* were transportable on bikes so that the *kamishibaiya* could easily ride around neighborhoods. This form of Japanese visual storytelling provided entertainment for both children and adults. Many *kamishibaiya* would later become *mangaka* (manga artists).

The sequence of events in *emakimono*, the monochrome and simple lines of *sumi-e*, the exaggerated facial expressions of *kabuki* actors, the woodblock-printed *kusazoshi* that brought entertainment to the masses, and *kamishibai*, which was an incubator for talented *mangaka*, all had an impact on the manga art form today. In many ways, it seems that *manga* evolved from a long history of Japanese visual storytelling. But we must also consider that in the 1850s, when Japan opened to the West, the people of Japan transitioned to the modern world, which had a huge impact on their society, technology, arts, and culture. Later, the development of manga was influenced by Western comics, as Japanese artists were looking to emulate the West and therefore adopted the style of cartooning and graphic narratives found in newspapers and other mediums. After WWII, the people of Japan were seeking affordable entertainment, and this led to the mass production of manga magazines and books. This demand for entertainment influenced the Japanese publishing industry and the manga that we now purchase for our libraries.

THE HISTORY OF MANGA

To learn more about the history of manga, read *Manga! Manga! The World of Japanese Comics*, by Frederik L. Schodt. This book dives into the culture of comics in Japan, as well as its origins, its evolution, and its value in a global market. You can also read *Comics and the Origins of Manga: A Revisionist History* by Eike Exner. This book challenges the idea that manga developed from traditional Japanese visual storytelling, and instead argues that manga was influenced by foreign comics. Also, check out *The Citi Exhibition: Manga* edited by Nicole Coolidge Rousmaniere and Matsuba Ryoko. This book will provide an understanding of Japanese visual storytelling and how to read, interpret, and analyze manga.

HOW TO READ MANGA

Many readers have experience reading Western comics, so they are likely comfortable with that style of visual storytelling. But for readers who are new to manga, there can be quite a challenging transition. Western comics are read from left-to-right, but the pages, panels, and text bubbles of manga are all meant to be read from right-to-left.

Manga Panels

When following the panels in a manga, start each page in the upper-right corner. Then move to the left to the next panel or move down to the following row of panels starting on the right. (See figure 1.1.) *Yonkoma* manga, or four-panel manga, is read by starting with the panel at the top of the page, then moving down to the next panel below.

Manga Text Bubbles

When following the text bubbles in manga, start each page in the upper-right corner of the upper right panel. The text bubbles should be read in a right-to-left and up-to-down order (see figure 1.2).

FIGURE 1.1 | **Manga Panels**

FIGURE 1.2 | **Manga Text Bubbles**

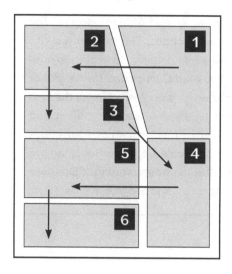

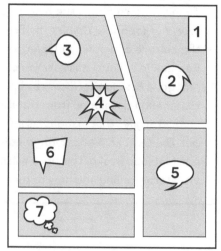

Manga Design Elements

Manga pages, panels, and text bubbles also have some very specific design elements. If the background of the panels is black, this implies a flashback to an earlier event, period, or time. Also, the design of the text bubble may indicate a variety of dialogue, thoughts, or narration. There are also a bunch of onomatopoetic sound effects that deserve attention.

Japanese Visual Language

Characters in manga are not only visually expressive through their dialogue, but also visually expressive with their emotions. Understanding Japanese Visual Language (JVL), the graphic representation and visual style in manga, can enhance one's reading experience. For example, an empty dialogue bubble under a character's mouth is a sigh of relief; lines on a character's cheeks indicate blushing; a nosebleed indicates lust; sweat drops indicate embarrassment or worry; a snot bubble coming out of a character's nose indicates sleeping; sharp teeth and popping veins indicate anger; heart-shaped eyes indicate love; water pouring out of a character's eyes indicates extreme joy or sadness; and so much more.

Supporting Manga Readers

If manga readers are struggling with their comprehension, ensure that they are reading the panels and the text bubbles in the correct sequential order. Also, provide readers with the opportunity to learn more about JVL and the unique visually storytelling style of manga.

MANGA READERSHIP

Like many books, manga is also often created to target a specific demographic of readers. These manga readerships are usually based on age and gender, and consist of *kodomo*, *shojo*, *shonen*, *josei*, and *seinen*.

Kodomo (child) is manga that targets all genders under the age of 10. These stories are usually about family and friends and often focus on having adventures and learning lessons. Examples of *kodomo* manga are *Pokémon Adventures*, *Yo-kai Watch*, and *Chi's Sweet Home*.

Shojo or *shoujo* (young girl) is manga that targets a female readership that is age 10 or older. *Shojo* manga often focuses on the development of interpersonal relationships between friends and family, as well as romantic relationships with a focus on trust and respect. *Shojo* manga also often focuses on personal growth, which includes exploring identities, self-acceptance, and empowerment. Examples of *shojo* manga are *Horimiya*, *My Love Mix-Up!* and *Monthly Girls' Nozaki-kun*.

Shonen (young boy) is manga that targets a male readership that is age 10 or older. *Shonen* manga often focuses on the hero's journey, which aligns with themes of heroism and bravery. *Shonen* manga also often focuses on how a character changes during this journey and on how the obstacles they face allow them to mature, demonstrate perseverance, and gain wisdom or power. Examples of *shonen* manga are *My Hero Academia*, *One Piece*, and *Jujutsu Kaisen*.

Josei (woman) is manga that targets a female readership that is age 18 or older. *Josei* was created to meet the needs and interests of mature women. *Josei* stories often focus on the experiences of women, including romance and relationships, careers and family life, and sex. Examples of *josei* manga are *Princess Jellyfish*, *Perfect World*, and *Wotakoi: Love Is Hard for Otaku*.

Seinen (youth) is manga that targets a male readership that is age 18 or older. *Seinen* was created to meet the needs and interests of mature men. *Seinen* stories can focus on action, fantasy, science fiction, or horror and can often include graphic violence or erotic scenes. Examples of *seinen* manga are *Berserk*, *Tokyo Ghoul*, and *Golden Kamuy*.

MANGA GENRES

Manga is enjoyable for many readers because of the wide variety of genres available. Having a variety of genres allows *mangaka* to create specific types of stories for specific types of readers. This consistency in manga genres allows readers to become familiar with a specific style, content, and themes and therefore able to know what to expect. This anticipation can help to build strong and confident readers. This confidence not only helps to build literacy skills, but also encourages a lifelong love of reading. Readers can develop the awareness and ability to identify the specific types of manga that they enjoy reading. They can also build connections to these stories and deeply engage in the reading experience. If readers have experience reading a particular genre, they can also decode and construct the meaning in manga titles of similar genres. Strong readers read a variety of genres. Reading a variety of genres can help build language, inspire imagination, and expand knowledge.

POPULAR MANGA GENRES

- Action
- Adventure
- Animals
- Art
- Cats
- Comedy
- Cooking
- Drama
- Dystopian
- Fairy Tales
- Fantasy

- Historical
- Horror
- *Isekai*
- *Kaiju*
- *Magical Girl*
- *Mecha*
- Music
- Mystery
- Romance
- School
- Science Fiction

- *Slice of Life*
- Sports
- Supernatural
- Superpowers
- Thriller
- Vampires
- Video Games
- Witches
- *Yaoi* (Boys' Love)
- *Yuri*

GENRES UNIQUE TO MANGA

While there are many manga genres that are consistent with the genres of fiction, there are also many others that are unique to manga. Some of these genres include *isekai, kaiju, magical girl, mecha, slice of life, yaoi,* and *yuri.*

Isekai refers to a genre of manga where a character is transported to or reborn in another world. Examples of *isekai* manga are *Ascendance of a Bookworm, I'm in Love with the Villainess,* and *So I'm a Spider, So What?*

Kaiju refers to a genre of manga that includes giant monsters with great powers like Godzilla. Examples of *kaiju* manga are *Kaiju No. 8, Kaiju Girl Caramelise,* and *Neon Genesis Evangelion.*

Magical girl refers to a genre of manga where female characters acquire magical abilities and must fight evil. Examples of *magical girl* manga are *Sailor Moon, Cardcaptor Sakura,* and *Little Witch Academia.*

Mecha refers to a genre of manga that includes large robotic machines like those in *Transformers.* Examples of *mecha* manga are *Mobile Suit Gundam, Knights of Sidonia,* and *Ultraman.*

Slice of Life refers to a genre of manga that focuses on everyday events of characters. Examples of *slice of life* manga are *The Way of the Househusband*, *Laid Back Camp*, and *Sweetness & Lightning*.

Yaoi (*Boys' love*) refers to a genre of manga that depicts intimate/romantic relationships between boys or men, usually written for a female audience. Examples of *yaoi* manga are *Our Dining Table*, *Given*, and *Sasaki and Miyano*.

Yuri refers to a genre of manga that depicts intimate/romantic relationships between girls or women. Examples of *yuri* manga are *Bloom into You*, *Whisper Me a Love Song*, and *Adachi and Shimamura*.

MANGA PUBLISHERS

Aside from becoming familiar with manga readerships and manga genres, it's also important to become familiar with manga publishers. On publishers' websites and social media accounts, you can find new releases, new series, top sellers, reviews, blurbs, age ratings, and more. Publishers' content and resources can help you build strong and varied collections of manga.

MANGA PUBLISHERS TO FOLLOW

Kodansha. Kodansha.us.
Kodansha publishes popular manga titles such as *Boys Run the Riot*, *Attack on Titan*, and *Witch Hat Atelier*. Kodansha also has other imprints and divisions, including the imprint Vertical (Japanese fiction, nonfiction, and manga).

VIZ Media. viz.com.
VIZ Media publishes popular manga titles such as *Naruto*, *Bleach*, and *Death Note*. VIZ Media also has other imprints and divisions, including Shonen Jump (*shonen* manga), VIZ Signature (manga for sophisticated readers), VIZ Originals (original content from manga-inspired creators), Shojo Beat (*shojo* manga), and SuBLime (*yaoi*/boys' love manga).

Seven Seas Entertainment. sevenseasentertainment.com.
Seven Seas Entertainment publishes popular manga titles such as *Nicola Traveling Around the Demons' World*, *Creepy Cat*, and *Our Dreams at Dusk*. Seven Seas Entertainment also has other imprints and divisions,

including Airship (light novels), Ghost Ship (sexually provocative content for mature readers), and Steamship (romantic *shojo* and *josei* titles).

Yen Press. Yenpress.com.

Yen Press publishes popular manga titles such as *I Want to Be a Wall*, *Bungo Stray Dogs*, and *Erased*. Yen Press also has other imprints and divisions, including JY (graphic novels for middle grades), IZE Press (Korean webcomics and novels), Yen On (light novels), and Yen Audio (audiobooks of light novels).

MANGA AGE RATINGS

Age ratings have been created by manga publishers to try and provide guidance to librarians, educators, and parents. While this is not a perfect system, it is a good starting point, especially if you are concerned about selecting age-appropriate and age-relevant manga titles for your library. In the end, it is ultimately the librarian's responsibility to make the final decisions about what manga to select. Furthermore, age ratings are usually found on the back cover of the print book where you can also find the blurb, on the last page of an e-book, and/or on the publisher's website.

STANDARD AGE RATINGS FOR MANGA

- All Ages
- 8+ or 10+
- 13+ or Teen
- 16+ or Teen Plus or Older Teen
- Mature

Each manga publisher might have a slightly different approach to their age ratings, including different age groups, different age rating names, and different criteria. Once you get a sense of the age ratings from each publisher, the language, the common themes and ideas, and what to expect from that publisher's content, it will become easier to determine which manga is the best fit for your community.

VIZ MEDIA AGE RATINGS

The following are the age ratings that VIZ Media has identified for its manga. Each category includes the specific age group and content criteria that they use to identify the intended reader.

All Ages: May be suitable for readers or consumers of any age. For example, may contain mild language and fantasy violence, but no swearing or nudity.

Teen: May be suitable for early teens and older. For example, may contain violence, infrequent use of strong language, suggestive themes or situations, crude humor, alcohol and/or tobacco use.

Teen Plus: May be suitable for older teens and adults. For example, may contain intense and/or gory violence, sexual content, frequent strong language, and alcohol, tobacco, and/or other substance use.

Mature: Suitable for adults only. May contain extreme violence, mature themes, and graphic depictions.

Source: VIZ Media, "Our Ratings," www.viz.com/ratings.

Within the description of the age ratings from VIZ Media, it clearly states that manga titles "may contain" this type of content. So, as a librarian be mindful that not all content will be present within a title with that specific age rating. All content could be included, some of it may be included, or it may not be included at all. So, identify what type of content meets the needs and interests of your community and move forward from there. The best way to ensure that you are making the best selections for your manga collection is to read manga, become a manga age-ratings expert, and put the needs and interests of your readers before your own biases.

Some publishers of manga also provide tools on their website that allow you to browse and filter through series by age ratings. For example, Yen Press organizes its titles by age ratings at yenpress.com/titles-by-rating, and Kodansha provides filters to browse their manga collection by age rating, genre, format, and status at kodansha.us/manga/browse-series.

CONTENT WARNINGS

Content warnings are not always listed within a manga, but in most of the print and digitally published manga by VIZ Media, there are parental advisory warnings. These parental advisory warnings are essentially content warnings that can help you identify whether to purchase the manga for your library community. To be able to use this information effectively, you must understand the content associated with that language. I searched through quite a lot of manga to identify patterns in VIZ Media's content warnings, and I noticed patterns for violence, sexuality, language, and ideas.

Violence

Violence in manga is one of the most common reasons for challenges and censorship. While violence can vary based on the age ratings of teen, older teen, and mature, it's important to know the difference between the levels of violence that can be found in manga. Violence can be defined as using physical force to intentionally injure, damage, or kill someone or something.

VIOLENCE CONTENT WARNINGS

- Depictions of Violence
- Realistic Violence
- Graphic Violence
- Fantasy Violence
- Blood
- Gore
- Death

Sometimes the acts of violence in manga can be realistic, such as bullying, fighting in battles, and the use of weapons. Sometimes acts of violence can be incredibly graphic and brutal, including mutilations, amputations, murder, suicide, and sexual violence. Fantasy violence usually consists of acts of violence that cannot occur in real life. These fantastical elements can include violence because of superpowers or the actions of vampires, ghouls, and demons. It should not be surprising to find that manga might include blood, gore, and viscera. There could also be some instances where aggressive actions toward a character end up harmless, with no resulting injury. Sometimes manga might not even include the act of violence, but only the results of violence, like the death of a character. When selecting manga that has content warnings for violence, you should consider the intended audience, the reader, and the community.

Sexuality

Sexuality in manga is another one of the most common reasons for challenges and censorship. Again, while sexuality can vary based on the age ratings of teen, older teen, and mature, you should know the difference between the levels of sexuality that can be found in manga. Sexuality can be defined as how a person expresses their sexual feelings through thoughts and behaviors.

SEXUALITY CONTENT WARNINGS

- Awkwardness of Youth
- First Love Shenanigans
- Teenage Relationships
- Suggestive Themes
- Nudity
- Suggestive Imagery
- Sexual Situations
- Sexual Themes
- Adult Themes

Sometimes the sexuality expressed in manga can range from innocent handholding to explicit sex. Thinking about the developmental age and maturity of your readers will allow you to make the best decisions for the titles in your manga collection. If you are collecting manga for teens, you should consider adding titles with first-love experiences and teenage relationships. Because manga often mirrors real life, try to identify content that celebrates self-discovery, budding sexuality, and healthy romantic relationships. The content warning suggestive themes and imagery usually means that while there is no explicit sex in the manga, there may be references to it through a character's words or actions, which could also include partial nudity. When it comes to suggestive content, the overall intention of the *mangaka* is to be provocative and allow the reader to think of sex. Titles for older teens may include more sexual situations and themes that may include kissing, touching, teasing, and nudity, whereas explicit sexual situations may often be found in titles rated mature.

Language and Ideas

There are also content warnings that pertain to language, which include mild language, strong language, adult humor, and crude humor. This could include insults and profanity, as well as jokes about genitalia and bodily functions. I also recently found systemic oppression as a content warning in a VIZ Media manga. Systemic oppression occurs when there are societal structures and laws in place that limit resource access and reinforce the unequal treatment of people in a specific group. Many characters in manga share similar experiences with the readers in our communities. While it is essential that these stories are represented and told, it is also important to note that the content in the story may be problematic and triggering.

TRANSLATION NOTES

While manga is originally published in Japan, its publishing companies hire translators to bring this content to American audiences. Translators do not just translate dialogue, thoughts, and sound effects but cultural events, values, traditions, and more. The goal is to provide American audiences with a reading experience that is akin to the original.

Oftentimes, translation notes can be found at the end of a manga and can support or enhance the reading experience. Translation notes give translators the opportunity to define any vocabulary and include any additional information that did not fit within the confines of the text bubbles in the manga. They also provide readers with additional information about things pertaining to Japanese language and culture. Sometimes in the back of manga, you can also find essays, short stories, biographies, interviews, character descriptions, recipes, manga recommendations, and more.

LIBRARIANS AND MANGA

There is a lot to learn about the history of manga, the evolution of manga, and the current popular trends in manga. Therefore, as a librarian, you should remain informed about manga and read manga. There is no greater connection that you can build with a reader than to share a celebrated love of reading. The authenticity of your knowledge and experience with manga will bring more readers to the library and keep more readers using the library.

MANGA COLLECTION DEVELOPMENT

MANGA SHOULD BE EASILY ACCESSIBLE TO ALL readers in the library community. There should be designated locations throughout the library for the manga collections, along with manga book displays, manga book lists, and a manga suggestion box. It is important to stay informed about manga bestsellers, high-circulating titles, and what new titles readers want to read. If you know the community, know the resources, and know the manga, you will be able to provide a robust manga reading culture in your library as well as limit challenges to manga.

MANGA COLLECTION DEVELOPMENT POLICY

Selecting manga for the library can be challenging, as budgets are limited and the demand for this medium can be high. To navigate these challenges, there needs to be a system in place that ensures you can prioritize and purchase manga that meet the needs and interests of your library's community. The goal of a manga collection development policy is to ensure that you have specific criteria and objectives to follow for building a manga collection, maintaining a manga collection, and handling a manga challenge.

QUESTIONS FOR A MANGA COLLECTION DEVELOPMENT POLICY

Consider the following questions about the library, the community, and the collection when creating a manga collection development policy.

Know the Library

- What is the mission of the library?
- What is the vision of the library?
- What are the goals of the library?
- What is the culture of the library?

Know the Community

- What are the ages of the patrons that the library serves?
- What are the demographics of the patrons that the library serves?
- What are the needs of the library community?
- What are the interests of the library community?

Know the Collection

- What manga titles are in the library collection?
- What audience does this collection serve?
- What publisher age ratings does the librarian consider?
- What professional resources does the librarian consider?

TIPS FOR MANGA COLLECTION DEVELOPMENT

Aside from creating a manga collection development policy, there are many other factors to consider when building a manga collection in the library. Some of these factors include limited budgets, supply chain issues, missing and out-of-print volumes, digital access, limited shelf space, extended series, and more.

Budgets can be managed by prioritizing titles and limiting the length of series in the collection, hosting fund-raising events, and applying for grants. If the library's budget is limited, consider reaching out to the Parent Teacher Association or the Friends of the Library to see if they can work collaboratively to host fundraising opportunities like bake sales, book fairs, or special programs. If you are a member of the American Library Association (ALA), the American Association of School Librarians (AASL), or the Young Adult Library Services Association (YALSA), there are quite a few annual grants available that could provide funding for collection development, including the AASL's Inspire Collection Development Grant and the ALA's Eisner Graphic Novel Grants for Libraries.

While supply chain issues and out-of-print titles are challenges that librarians may always face, the supply chain issues will eventually improve, and searching used book websites and stores for out-of-print titles is always an adventure. Regarding missing volumes in a manga series, you can purchase multiple copies of volumes in a popular series, keep a tracker of what missing volumes to purchase when the budget allows, and supplement the physical collection with a digital collection.

Limited shelf space can be resolved by weeding and shifting the library collection, rotating manga series, and finding unique ways to display titles. Also, when considering the organization of the library shelves, you can organize the manga collection by title and volume. Providing digital access to the manga collection also allows you to immediately purchase new releases, fill the gaps in your collection, continue extended series when shelf space is limited, and avoid supply chain issues. You could also check with the administration to see if there is software or technology funding available, outside of the library's budget, for e-books with Sora or a digital subscription with ComicsPlus.

BUILDING A MANGA COLLECTION

My school library has over 250 manga series in its collection, titles that I have spent time reading, questioning, and considering. While there are hundreds of manga series that can be purchased for a library, here are some of my suggestions for starting a collection. Please keep in mind that these manga titles are in a library collection that serves students, grades 6–12, in New York City. Therefore, the titles that meet the needs and interests of my library community may not meet the needs and interests of another library community. So, still plan to vet these titles by checking age ratings and reviews and considering your library's manga collection development policy. The following list is organized by age rating and then title:

My Neighbor Seki by Takuma Morishige. Vertical Comics. 8+
  Rumi is a diligent student who wants to focus and be successful in all her classes. But she has a pesky classmate named Seki, who sits next to her and distracts her. Often Rumi tries to get him to concentrate on class by trying to disrupt his antics. Sometimes she tries to ignore him, but the elaborate and hilarious games Seki plays at his desk almost always capture her attention.

Penguin & House by Akiho Ieda. Kodansha. 8+

Pen is a penguin. But he is no ordinary penguin. He can read, knit, play baseball, go food shopping, cook dinner and dessert, do the laundry, clean, and so much more. . . . Pen lives with his human "keeper," Hayakawa. When Pen's keeper is away at school, Pen is at home thinking of all the ways that he can express his love for Hayakawa.

Creepy Cat by Cotton Valent. Seven Seas Entertainment. 10+

When Flora first moves into a mansion she inherits, she feels like she is being watched. She then comes to find that something already lives there: Creepy Cat, a white, round feline with red eyes. Creepy Cat seems like a regular cat but he can float, move through walls, multiply himself, shape-shift, and more. They become friends and the story follows scenes from their daily lives together, full of cute but troublesome pranks and dangerous adventures.

The Girl from the Other Side by Nagabe. Seven Seas Entertainment. 13+

In this faraway land, there are two realms: the Inside, where humans live in peace and are protected by the light, and the Outside, where cursed beasts roam in the darkness. One day Shiva, a human girl, is found on the Outside by a horned demon she comes to call Teacher. He takes care of her and the two become family, but as the story continues some truths from darkness come to light.

A Silent Voice by Yoshitoki Oima. Kodansha. 13+

When Shoyo was growing up, he was mean and pressured his friends into making poor choices. He also targeted and bullied Shoko, a young girl with a hearing disability. His torment went too far, and Shoko left school to make a fresh start somewhere else. Years later, as a high schooler, Shoyo is depressed and feels a lot of regret. Then by chance, he meets up with Shoko again, and this time he tries to make it up to her, any way he can.

Wandance by Coffee. Kodansha. 13+

Kaboku likes to keep quiet and doesn't like to draw attention to himself because life as a teen is hard enough without also having to worry about a stutter. One day, after school, he sees a girl named Wanda dancing. She is alone and doesn't seem to care if anyone is watching. Then something comes alive within Kaboku. He too wants to feel the freedom that Wanda feels, so he decides to join the dance club.

your name. **by Makoto Shinkai and Ranmaru Kotone. Yen Press. 13+**

Taki is a high school boy from Tokyo, and Mitsuha is a high school girl who lives in the mountains of Japan. The two begin to have dreams that they are living the life of another person. They soon realize that these are not dreams; they are swapping lives and sharing bodies. As their stories begin to weave together, they begin to discover more about each other. Then they realize they have developed a bond and desperately want to hold on to one another.

Blue Lock **by Muneyuki Kaneshiro and Yusuke Nomura. Kodansha. 16+**

After Japan fails to win the World Cup, the soccer community is determined to fix "the problem" and find the best striker in Japan. They take 300 of the best soccer players in the country and send them to a state-of-the-art training facility named Blue Lock. The goal is to have groups of players compete against each other in tournaments until there is one man left standing—the one who will become the striker for Japan's national soccer team.

The Promised Neverland **by Kaiu Shirai and Posuka Demizu. VIZ Media. 16+**

This story is about a group of children who were raised in an orphanage. But after discovering the awful truth surrounding the purpose of their existence and what happens when they are "adopted" . . . they plan their escape. This escape is met with a series of challenges that are both exciting and terrifying. But the children learn about sacrifice, determination, and the value and meaning of freedom.

Tokyo Ghoul **by Sui Ishida. VIZ Media. 16+**

In this world there are ghouls that look like humans, but they need to eat human flesh to survive. These ghouls must hide their true identities and live in secrecy among the human population. Kaneki, a student who barely survives a ghoul attack, learns that he had a surgery that turned him into a half-ghoul. As he struggles with his new identity, he must also learn to deal with his new life, and his new urge to eat human flesh.

LOOKING FOR MORE SUGGESTED MANGA TITLES?

The Manga in Libraries website (MangaInLibraries.com) includes manga collection development lists for all ages, teens, and older teens that are updated frequently. The table below provides a brief review of some of the titles that you can find from the lists on MangaInLibraries.com.

All Ages

Ascendance of a Bookworm | Cardcaptor Sakura | Cat Massage Therapy | The Evil Secret Society of Cats | Little Witch Academia

Lovely Muco! | My Neighbor Totoro | A Polar Bear in Love | Splatoon | Yokai Watch

Teens

Bleach | Dr. Stone | The Elusive Samurai | Erased | Horimiya

Kaguya-sama: Love Is War | Kaiju No. 8 | My Love Mix-Up! | A Tropical Fish Yearns for Snow | Toilet-Bound Hanako-kun

Older Teens

Asadora! — Attack on Titan — Beauty and the Beast of Paradise Lost — Blue Period — Death Note

Look Back — Perfect World — Rooster Fighter — A Sign of Affection — The Way of the Househusband

RESOURCES FOR MANGA COLLECTION DEVELOPMENT

With the constant release of new manga titles, it is important to stay up to date. Aside from reading manga and asking readers for recommendations, there are quite a few other resources that you can use to find engaging, appropriate, and relevant manga titles for your library collections.

Manga Resources

The Graphic Library. graphiclibrary.org.
This website provides reviews of manga and graphic novels for librarians.

Graphic Novels & Comics Round Table (GNCRT). "Best Graphic Novels Reading Lists." ala.org/rt/gncrt/awards/best-graphic-novels-reading-lists.
Provided annually, the GNCRT shares the best graphic novels for adults and children. The recommended titles include manga.

Manga in Libraries. "Lists." mangainlibraries.com/book-lists.
    The manga title lists available on Manga in Libraries are broken down into several categories of age groups (all ages, teens, and older teens), and there are also recommendation lists for teaching with manga, social-emotional learning, disability visibility, and more.

Mangasplaining **(podcast). mangasplaining.com.**
    This is a podcast dedicated to manga with episodes that include recommendations of manga to read.

No Flying No Tights. noflyingnotights.com.
    On this website, you can browse manga and graphic novel titles by age recommendations, genres, and starred reviews.

YALSA. "Great Graphic Novels for Teens List." ala.org/yalsa/ great-graphic-novels.
    Updated annually, this list shares the best teen graphic novels of the year. Its recommended titles include manga.

Manga Bookstores

Here are a few bookstores to browse for manga collection development:
- Barnes & Noble (bookstore with a manga collection)
- BookOff (Japanese used bookstore)
- Forbidden Planet (comic shop with a manga collection)
- Kinokuniya (Japanese bookstore)
- The Strand (used bookstore with a manga collection)

MANGA CONTENT CREATORS

Some manga content creators have created resources that can support librarians with expert information about manga collection development. The following interviews allowed me the chance to connect with some of these creators. The goal of these interviews was to learn about the resources they have created, how those resources can support librarians with manga collection development, and what titles librarians should purchase for their manga collections. These resources will allow you to offer manga collections that can best support the needs and interests of everyone in your library community.

MANGASPLAINING
An Interview with Deb Aoki

Deb Aoki (she/her) is a lifelong comics reader and fourth-generation Japanese American who grew up in Honolulu, Hawaii, surrounded by Asian pop culture, including manga, anime and *tokusatsu* (live action superhero) shows. She writes about manga for *Publishers Weekly* and is one-quarter of the weekly podcast *Mangasplaining* (mangasplaining .com), a show that introduces manga to "people who haven't read much manga before," with co-hosts Chip Zdarsky, Christopher Butcher, and David Brothers. Deb is also a comics creator, user experience designer, and illustrator based in Oakland, California.

Q: How can *Mangasplaining* support librarians with building a manga collection?

A: We started *Mangasplaining* because we know there are a lot of comics readers, librarians, comic and book shop retailers, and publishing professionals who are curious about manga, but find it intimidating to get into it. On *Mangasplaining*, we offer discussion and detailed show notes that provide even new readers with background info and cultural context for the manga we spotlight, to make it accessible for anyone who is just looking for something fun to read. I think we're a good source of information about manga for people who aren't deeply immersed in its culture or history. We discuss a broad range of stories and art styles, for tween, teen, and adult readers. We love manga, and we hope that this show helps more people discover manga as a source of fascinating stories about almost every subject for almost every reader.

Q: Librarians often ask, where do I start my collection? What suggestions do you have for starting a manga collection?

A: Where do you start a manga collection? I guess my best recommendation is to ask your patrons for what they're interested in! Your patrons will tell you what they want to read, so ask them and dig in. You might find that some of what they want is maybe not appropriate for their age group—but listen anyway, because you'll start noticing trends about what's hot and what's not.

23

Start watching anime! A lot of what drives readers' interest in manga is whatever anime is currently airing on Crunchyroll, Netflix, or Hulu. Watching an anime series will give you a taste of what the story is about and whether its content is appropriate for your students.

There are, of course, titles that are perennial favorites that almost every library with even the most basic manga collection should have. If I had to pick just a handful of must-buy titles, I'd recommend the following titles (which are organized by age and then alphabetically by title):

- *Yotsuba&!* by Kiyohiko Azuma. Yen Press. All ages
Yotsuba is a green-haired little girl who, along with her father, moves to a new town. Every day is fun for this curious preschooler as she discovers something new, meets someone, or does something she's never done before. This 's a charming, slice-of-life series that is often hilarious and is a delightful read for all ages.

- *Chi's Sweet Home* by Kanata Konami. Kodansha. 10+
Chi is a mischievous kitten who gets separated from his mama and siblings, and then is adopted by a couple and their preschool-age son. The problem is, they live in an apartment complex that doesn't allow pets! This is a sweet and fun series that explains the joys and challenges of pet ownership.

- *Sailor Moon* by Naoko Takeuchi. Kodansha. 10+
This is not the first, but is probably the most popular "magical girl" manga series around, and it is one that continues to enchant generation after generation of readers. Usagi is a cute and kind of klutzy girl, but when she awakens to her destiny, she and her friends become superpowered guardians with magical powers who battle the forces of evil. Full of adventure, magic, and romance, this series is a must-read for anyone who loves manga.

- *Witch Hat Atelier* by Kamome Shirahama. Kodansha. 10+
A young girl discovers the secret of magic, and after a spell goes wrong, she is taken in by a teacher who mentors her and three other fledgling witches about what it takes and what the cost of wielding magical powers is.

■ *Fruits Basket* by Natsuki Takaya. Yen Press. 13+

After her mother dies, Tohru finds a job as a housekeeper for the very rich and very odd Sohma family. Their secret: some of them turn into animals when they have contact with a member of the opposite sex. This series starts out as a wacky fantasy comedy, but in later volumes it turns into a touching story about overcoming dysfunctional families and learning to love again.

■ *My Hero Academia* by Kohei Horikoshi. VIZ Media. 13+

In a world where almost everyone has a "quirk" or special power, Izuku has none. But a fateful encounter with the world's strongest and most famous hero leads Izuku to enroll in an exclusive school for aspiring heroes. This is a top-selling current series that is middle-school friendly and offers a bridge between superhero comics and manga.

■ *My Love Story!* by Kazune Kawahara and Aruko. VIZ Media. 13+

Takeo is strong and kind-hearted, but he's also a big, burly guy who isn't your typical high school heartthrob. But when he falls in love he falls *hard*, and who couldn't help but love a guy who's just so determined to succeed? A funny and heart-warming romance.

■ *Naruto* by Masashi Kishimoto. VIZ Media. 13+

In this series, a boy ninja who is possessed by the spirit of a nine-tailed fox demon aspires to be the greatest ninja of his village—but he's got a long way to go to meet this goal, especially since most of his village thinks he's either a pest or someone who will grow up to fulfill a dangerous destiny. This is an epic adventure that will enthrall readers from tweens to teens and beyond.

■ *One Piece* by Eiichiro Oda. VIZ Media. 13+

This is one of the longest-running and perennially popular manga out there today. When Luffy eats the Gum-Gum fruit, he gains the power to be a rubber man: to make his limbs stretch and bend to do incredible feats. With this power, he sets out to become the king of the pirates. With the help of friends he meets along the way, Luffy and the Straw Hat Pirates travel the world and have incredible adventures that just get more fun and exciting with every volume.

■ *Ranma ½* by Rumiko Takahashi. VIZ Media. 16+

This is a funny, gender-bending, slapstick martial arts comedy about a boy who turns into a girl when he's splashed with cold water, and the various eccentrics who either want to fight him or go out with him/her, or maybe sometimes both.   */////*

THE GRAPHIC LIBRARY
An Interview with Sara Smith

Sara Smith (she/her) is a teacher librarian at a high school in California. She is an avid reader and reviewer of graphic novels for school libraries. She writes reviews for her website, The Graphic Library (graphiclibrary .org) and is also a manga reviewer for *Booklist* magazine. Her work has also appeared in *Booklist Reader*, *Diamond Bookshelf*, and *California English*. She has appeared on the podcasts *School Librarians United* and *The Secret Stacks* discussing graphic novels, especially manga.

Q: How can The Graphic Library support librarians with building a manga collection?

A: The Graphic Library is a review website, to help librarians select graphic novels for their library collections. In my district, our selection policy requires a title to be positively reviewed by a professional in the library field. Graphic novels have not historically been given a lot of space in professional magazines, and manga even less so. It seemed like the magazines were focusing more on what I'd call "literary" graphic novels, but readers want comics and manga. Additionally, these publications have limited space to publish reviews, so there are only so many titles per month that will "make the cut," so to speak. I decided that I wanted to create a space to provide professional reviews through the lens of a teacher librarian in a school setting, and I could post as many or as few reviews as I wanted without having to worry about how many pages were in the publication.

Q: Librarians often ask, where do I start my collection? What suggestions do you have for starting a manga collection?
A: I believe that a fundamental job of every librarian is to find a book for every reader. If you don't have a diverse collection, complete with a robust manga collection, you're certainly not going to match up every reader with a book. Here are a few suggestions for manga titles that cover a range of genres and support a range of readers, from elementary school to high school. (This book list is organized by age, then alphabetically by title.)

■ *The Fox and Little Tanuki* by Tagawa Mi. TokyoPop. All ages
Senzou was a terribly powerful magical beast who now must serve a penance of raising a little tanuki to be a good servant of the gods. This is a classic odd-couple comedy with cute Disney-type animals.

■ *Nicola Traveling Around the Demons' World* by Asaya Miyanaga. Seven Seas Entertainment. All ages
Nicola is a human girl and a struggling witch, saved by the demon Simon, who now finds herself traveling incognito in the Demon World, where humans aren't allowed.

■ *Pokémon* by Hidenori Kusaka. VIZ Media. All ages
Pokémon is an adventure story following "trainers," young people who capture creatures known as Pokémon and train them to compete in various tournaments.

■ *Demon Slayer* by Koyoharu Gotouge. VIZ Media. 13+
Tanjiro's family is attacked by demons, and his sister begins to transition into a demon. He seeks out renowned Demon Slayers to help him save his sister, but along the way, he decides to join their ranks and rid the world of these malicious creatures.

■ *Fullmetal Alchemist* by Hiromu Arakawa. VIZ Media. 13+
The Elric brothers travel their country of Amestris searching for a way to restore their original bodies after an alchemical experiment to bring back their mother goes awry.

■ *Haikyu!!* by Haruichi Furudate. VIZ Media. 13+
Hinata is obsessed with playing volleyball, but his junior high does not have much of a team. Once he gets into high school, he gets involved in the school's heavily competitive volleyball club.

■ *One-Punch Man* by ONE and Yusuke Murata. VIZ Media. 13+
Saitama trains to become a superhero, and he does so well that now he can defeat all manner of bad guys with one punch. Superhero work is kind of boring . . . . He joins the Hero Association so he can get jobs saving people, but still, nothing's very challenging.

■ *Ouran High School Host Club* by Bisco Hatori. VIZ Media. 13+
Haruhi accidentally breaks an expensive vase in the Host Club room and must work off her debt by becoming the errand boy for the Hosts. The Host Club specializes in entertaining female students with tea and sweets. This series is funny and caters to the "shipping" crowd of readers who want to play matchmaker with different characters.

■ *Jujutsu Kaisen* by Gege Akutami. VIZ Media. 16+
One day, Itadori and his friends discover a cursed object, a severed finger, and awaken a demon. Sorcerers from the Jujutsu Academy try to clean up the mess, but Itadori eats the finger and discovers that, instead of being killed, he can control the demon it belonged to.

■ *Spy x Family* by Tatsuya Endo. VIZ Media. 16+
Loid, codenamed Twilight, is a super-spy and a master of disguise, and he is completely dedicated to his job. His latest assignment requires him to get close to his target through the use of a family, something Loid does not want to do. Enter Anya, a charming young telepath and Loid's "daughter," and Yor, an assassin and Loid's "wife," along with a host of hilarious supporting characters.   /////

MANGA CHALLENGES

Manga is a visual medium and can therefore be the target of challenges. Common misconceptions are that manga is too graphic, violent, and sexual. While some manga titles do include violence and sexuality, that is not to say that all titles do, or even do so in a graphic manner. These misconceptions, and others, usually lead challengers to seek the removal of a manga title from the library collection. Unfortunately, this action seeks to prevent access to the manga title for all readers. Since manga titles cannot be arbitrarily removed from the library collection, these challenges need to be handled with care.

But there is no one answer regarding how to handle a manga challenge; it depends on the community, the collection, and the challenge itself. Every library should create local resources for handling challenges, and every librarian who purchases manga should be prepared to face a challenge. If you understand the medium, understand its value, and are willing to fight for readers' right to read, then you are ready to handle a manga challenge in your library.

Tips for Preventing a Manga Challenge

Know your community. Consider the age and demographics of your readers, their needs and interests, and the library's mission and vision statements.

Create a collection development policy. Identify the purpose and educational value of the manga collection. Include some of the literacy skills and social-emotional benefits of manga in the policy.

Outline your guidelines for selecting manga. Define the criteria that are used for selecting manga. Include information about the medium, manga publisher ratings, and professional resources.

Know your manga collection. Be prepared to defend the manga in your library's collection. Create a spreadsheet that includes titles, age ratings, genres, and themes of the manga in the collection.

Tips for Handling for a Manga Challenge

Have a documented process for handling a manga challenge. Libraries should create a form for those wanting to challenge manga. The form should require the following: the challenger's contact information, and the title, *mangaka*, and publisher of the manga being challenged. Libraries should also require that the challenger read the manga and detail their concerns about the manga on the form.

Have a documented process for the reconsideration of a manga title. Libraries should be prepared to organize a committee that consists of a librarian, an educator/community member, an administrator/manager, and the challenger. After the challenger completes the form, this committee should meet, draw up possible solutions, and once a decision is made, create a written response of the action taken.

Libraries can also reach out to the ALA's Office for Intellectual Freedom for support with handling challenges to library materials. You can visit their website for more information: ala.org/tools/challengesupport.

ADVOCATING FOR MANGA

Advocating for the inclusion of manga in your library collections can help to reduce the barriers to accessing manga. Challengers should be informed that manga helps readers on their path to self-discovery and helps them to become empathetic members of their community. Also, you can inform challengers that the manga collection went through a thoughtful selection process and that all titles meet the needs and interests of the library community. Ensuring that readers have access to manga and enjoyable reading experiences is at the heart of our work as librarians.

REPRESENTATION IN MANGA

DIVERSE AND INCLUSIVE REPRESENTATION IN manga matters to our readers and the communities that we serve. Having a collection of manga in your library with positive representation can help to reduce the stereotypes of marginalized groups. Manga can help readers to experience different stories and perspectives and allow them to truly see, understand, and accept one another. This inclusion in manga can also provide validation and support for readers who often feel misunderstood and underrepresented in other media. Relevant and relatable stories and characters in manga that reflect the identities of readers can also increase their self-esteem, well-being, and pride.

EQUITY, DIVERSITY, AND INCLUSION

According to ALA, "Equity, diversity, and inclusion are fundamental values of the association and its members."[1] Therefore, as librarians, we need to ensure that we provide equitable access to a manga collection, programs, resources, and services that are diverse and inclusive. It is fundamental that we provide this equitable access to everyone within our communities. To effectively remove barriers, empower, and meet the needs of the diverse populations that we serve, we should continue to developing our knowledge of these communities and the manga titles, programs, resources, and services that will respectfully support them.

EXPERTS FROM THE FIELD

Over the years, I have been fortunate enough to meet some incredible experts from the field who have helped me to improve my knowledge and my practice. The following interviews gave me the chance to connect with some of these experts, who just so happen to also be amazing advocates of manga. These advocates reflect the diversity and the voices of our readers and communities. The goal of these interviews is to allow these experts to share their ideas about a manga topic that they are personally connected to and passionate about, so that librarians can continue to learn how to thoughtfully provide equitable access to diverse and inclusive manga that supports the needs of all members of our communities.

LGBTQ+ REPRESENTATION IN MANGA
An Interview with Erica Friedman

Erica Friedman (she/they) is an independent manga researcher and the author of *By Your Side: The First 100 Years of Yuri Anime and Manga*. She has edited manga for JManga, Seven Seas, and Udon Entertainment, most recently Riyoko Ikeda's epic historical classic, *The Rose of Versailles*. Erica has written about *yuri* manga for the Japanese literary journal *Eureka*, *Animerica* magazine, the Comic Book Legal Defense Fund, and Dark Horse.

Q: Why does positive representation in manga matter to our readers and to our communities?
A: As humans, we're always looking to see ourselves reflected in that great mirror we call "society." For a lot of reasons, most of history has only reflected an incredibly small segment of society back at us. Everyone else not reflected in that segment has found ways to create narratives in-between and around those reflections that fit our needs, but it's not the same. For people to just see themselves and people like them is an incredible gift. It validates and grounds people in their own existence and gives them a leg up to tell even more and better stories.

Q: How do manga creators illustrate positive representations of the LGBTQ+ community?

A: *Yuri* manga can educate a mainstream audience, can create allies in the non-queer readers who enjoy it, and most of all, can be that mirror for the queer folks out there who want to read about people like themselves. Right now, we're seeing more *yuri* that take on topics of ability, sexuality, gender, and mental and physical health. There are just so many ways to be as a human and having this represented and normalized within any subset is a great way to build empathy and intersectional communication.

Q: Can you think of a particular time when a manga reader felt represented in manga, when they personally connected with the story or a character?

A: I get comments and e-mails all the time from people who found *yuri* and were blown away by the idea that an entire genre exists that tells stories about women who love women. I was recently told by a bookseller that when she suggested my book to a young woman, this formerly shy girl really opened up about the kinds of books and media she was looking for . . . the bookseller was thrilled to be able to introduce her to all kind of queer manga!

I'm also often approached by parents of kids who read queer manga, who ask me how they should relate to it. I'm always glad to tell a parent or grandparent how they can be supportive, and not make assumptions.

Q: What resources could librarians access to continue their professional development, to learn more about supporting the LGBTQ+ community through manga?

A: Keep an eye on YouTube for panels at conventions that cover boys' love and *yuri* manga. A lot of them will talk about the research in these areas, as well as titles of interest. My Yuri Studio channel is where I talk about the history of *yuri*, and the Japan Foundation did a terrific series on "girls' culture" of Japan and the literature, manga, and anime inspired by it.

Q: What manga titles would you recommend that have positive representations of the LGBTQ+ community?
A: I would recommend the following titles:

Even Though We're Adults by Takako Shimura (Seven Seas)
In this series, a lesbian falls for a married woman and everything is complicated, but it's all very well-drawn and written in a way that is beautifully honest.

How Do We Relationship by Tamifull (VIZ Media)
Two college-age women fall in love, date, break up, and move on in this incredibly realistic portrayal of the life of two young women.

I'm in Love with the Villainess, story by Inori, art by Aonoshimo (Seven Seas)
This series is a high-fantasy *isekai* that has overt, positive, and honest queer representation.

My Wandering Warrior Existence by Kabi Nagata (Seven Seas)
This is a comic essay about gender, sexuality, mental health, and human relationships.

Sex Education 120% by Kikiki Tataki (Yen Press)
This series is a school life comedy based on the idea of a health teacher in high school actually talking about sexuality and gender.   /////

REPRESENTATION OF GIRLS AND WOMEN IN MANGA
An Interview with Laura Neuzeth

Laura Neuzeth (she/her) is a Mexican American online video content creator and social media influencer from California. Laura creates YouTube and TikTok content about *josei* and *shoujo* manga, manga recommendations, and reviews. Apart from creating manga content, Laura also enjoys creating content about anime, rhythm games, and cosplay. You can find her on YouTube, TikTok, Twitter, and Instagram at @lauraneuzeth.

Q: Why does positive representation in manga matter to our readers and to our communities?

A: Positive representation matters in any form of media, including manga. For many people (myself included), manga is the form of media they consume the most because of the storytelling style, artwork, and variety of stories. While I enjoy reading all types of stories, the ones that I resonate with the most are those that have positive representations of females and marginalized groups. It not only makes me feel more attached to that piece of work, but it also brings people who feel the same way to my online community. This has been the way that I've grown my online community the last two years. I've enjoyed getting the opportunity to talk to different people about why they connect to certain stories; sometimes hearing more about why someone relates to a certain series will make me appreciate the story more.

Q: How do manga creators illustrate positive representations of girls and women?

A: Manga has created a safe space for both female creators and fans to enjoy a form of media that was very much seen as something for "boys." For female writers, *shoujo* magazines in Japan have created a space for them to create the stories they want to put out. Whether they want to create more high school romances or give us something new and different, they have the space to do so and an audience that is willing to read those stories.

Manga in recent years has done an incredible job of celebrating and portraying different kinds of girls and women. We have strong and intelligent female leads like Shirayuki from the series *Snow White with the Red Hair* who's a court herbalist. We also have physically and emotionally strong and compassionate girls like Fumi from the series *QQ Sweeper* and *Queen's Quality* who's a high school girl who is wise beyond her years. We also have independent women who are praised for marching to the beat of their own drummer like Kyoko Mogami from the series *Skip Beat!*, which just celebrated its twentieth-year anniversary.

Q: Can you think of a particular time when a manga reader felt represented in manga, when they personally connected with the story or a character?
A: The first time I read something where I connected deeply to a character was when I read the first volume of *Sweat and Soap* by Kintetsu Yamada. While this wasn't the first time in media where I'd seen an introverted and shy girl as the female lead, it was one of the first that did not give her this grand makeover or change her in a way that would make her more appealing to the male gaze. Asako Yaeshima is a woman in her mid-twenties who is insecure about her sweating and scent, she's been bullied and teased about this since her childhood, and one of the few things that has brought her comfort are the soaps made by the company she ends up working for as an adult.

Throughout the 11-volume series, you do see Asako make changes to her physical appearance and her personality, but those changes are not forced upon her. She is also not forced to change to make herself more attractive for her boyfriend, which was something I found very refreshing. One of the instances where I felt deeply connected to her was when she bought a blue scrunchie for her hair, which to most people (including her brother) seemed like an insignificant thing. That blue scrunchie was one of the few things she did for herself, and the act of buying something that was bright and eye-catching when she was content and used to hiding in the background was something that brought back memories of me making gradual changes to not hide in the background. The entire series does a great job of illustrating that even adults have a lot of room for personal growth.

Q: What resources could librarians access to continue their professional development, to learn more about positive representations of girls and women through manga?
A: There are some great social media influencers in the *shoujo/josei* community who are doing incredible work educating people about these demographics and who also focus on positive representations of girls and women through manga.
- Colleen Carney (of Colleen's Manga Recs) is a non-binary YouTube and TikTok creator who is incredibly knowledgeable and passionate about *shoujo* manga.

- Christy Lou makes videos on YouTube and TikTok about the importance of demographics and has an incredible in-depth video about manga magazines.
- Another one of my favorite resources is Shoujosei News & Info on Twitter, which does daily posts about ongoing and upcoming *shoujo* manga series, recommendations, and informational graphics.
- And lastly, there's also my TikTok and YouTube accounts, where I share educational manga content, manga reviews, and recommendations. I'm very proud of the worst I've done but will always give credit where credit is due.

Q: What manga titles would you recommend that have positive representations of girls and women?
A: Some of my other favorites are considered classic *shoujo* series like *Kimi ni Todoke, Fruits Basket, Sailor Moon*, and *Cardcaptor Sakura*. All these classic series feature young girls who are empathetic, compassionate, and strong.

For the older crowd, *Sweat and Soap* offers incredible representation of women, and I will always continue to hype up that series. *A Sign of Affection* and *Perfect World* are two other series that offer positive representations of women, with *A Sign of Affection* bringing us an incredible female lead who is deaf. *Yuri* series like *Doughnuts under a Crescent Moon, Still Sick*, and *Even Though We're Adults* also provide great representations of adult women who are still making self-discoveries. /////

DISABILITY REPRESENTATION IN MANGA
An Interview with Victoria Rahbar

Victoria Rahbar (she/her, Mx.) is a PhD student at the University of British Columbia's School of Information. She earned a master of arts degree in East Asian studies from Stanford University and an MLIS degree from the University of Washington. She applies her manga studies research to the needs of libraries, continuously advocating for queer stories and disability representation.

Q: Why does positive representation in manga matter to our readers and to our communities?

A: In a barrier-ridden world where stories about disability are painfully absent in all mediums—not just manga—the central matter becomes one of fulfilling one of library science's most basic principles, "Every person his, her, or their book." Others may argue for the need for disability manga as either an educational tool or a social justice endeavor first, but my focus remains on serving disabled patrons. Caricature-free visibility allows readers to connect these stories to their own lives, a reading experience necessary for all patrons who enter our libraries. Accordingly, positive representation in disability manga must be acutely realistic, often relatable, and not inspiration porn.

Q: How do manga creators illustrate positive representations of disability?

A: Manga creators often draw on their own lived experience to write either autobiographical stories or those featuring fictional characters with similar experiences. In *Shino Can't Say Her Name*, *mangaka* Shuzo Oshimi shows that the excitement of starting high school is often marred by anxiety around self-introductions. When the protagonist Shino stands to address her class for the first time, her attempt is met with laughter. This honest depiction of first-day stressors is relatable to both those who may have dysphemia and those who do not, which follows Oshimi's personal goal of making manga that can connect with anyone.

Q: Can you think of a particular time when a manga reader felt represented in manga, when they personally connected with the story or a character?

A: Most people do not know what dyscalculia, dysgraphia, and even dyslexia are, so to see my life illustrated in Monzusu's *My Brain Is Different: Stories of ADHD and Other Developmental Disorders* shocked and comforted me. Monzusu's episodic manga essays, gathered from letters from real people, cover a wide range of neurodiverse stories, and establish that for some people neurodiversity is a disability, while for others it is not. Caitlin Moore reflects on her reading experience for the Anime News Network: "Several times while reading *My Brain Is Different*, I had to put the book down simply because I was so emotionally overwhelmed by seeing experiences so similar to my own on the page. When I finished reading, I spent half an hour in bed, quietly sobbing at how Monzusu discussed how things were changing and expressed her hopes for the future for people with developmental disorders."

Q: What resources could librarians access to continue their professional development, to learn more about supporting disabled patrons through manga?
A: Disability manga is an emerging genre, so resources are currently in development rather than already established.
- For a scholastic approach, check out *Reframing Disability in Manga* by Yoshiko Okuyama.
- CripCon's bibliography titled *Readings and Resources on Disability and Comic Books, Graphic Novels, and Manga* lists over twenty pages of recommendations.
- For book reviews, search by theme or title, with attention to reviews written by community members.
- Lastly, the language around disability is always shifting, so I recommend two resources before creating book displays and other materials. They are the *Disability Language Style Guide* from the National Center on Disability and Journalism and Emily Ladau's *Demystifying Disability*.

Q: What manga titles would you recommend that have positive representations of people with disabilities?
- *I Hear the Sunspot* by Yuki Fumino (deaf-hearing relationships)
- *March Comes in like a Lion* by Chica Umino (chronic illness and mental wellness)
- *Perfect World* by Rie Aruga (disabled–nondisabled relationships)
- *Real* by Takehiko Inoue (parasports)   */////*

BIPOC REPRESENTATION IN MANGA
An Interview with Renee Scott

Renee Scott (she/her) is a young adult librarian based in New York City, as well as a reviewer for the blog Good Comics for Kids. A dedicated *otaku* and gamer, Renee is a lifelong fan of comics, anime, and manga. She can be found on Twitter at @libraryladynyc, and on her review blog, The Library Lady of NYC Reviews.

Q: Why does positive representation in manga matter to our readers and to our communities?

A: We all want to see our stories in a positive light: something that builds respect and understanding not only for readers of all ages and backgrounds, but also for marginalized communities that have been ignored or portrayed negatively. Personally, I have a well-known love/hate relationship with the *Dragonball* series. While I understand why it's popular, and I'll be a fan of Piccolo forever, Mr. Popo and other stereotypically drawn characters rub me the wrong way. Constantly seeing those images being celebrated always hurts my soul—especially the Sister Krone character from *The Promised Neverland*. While her anime counterpart is somewhat better, how she was drawn in the manga was the worst thing I've seen in a long time; it was so bad that a teen boy used her manga image to bully a Black teen girl in front of me! So, representation does matter in order to prevent instances like that from happening again.

Q: How do manga creators illustrate positive representations of BIPOC characters?

A: We're seeing more relatable storylines and respectful images of the BIPOC community, which had eluded us decades ago. Seeing stories of characters living in single-parent homes (like I did) and overcoming adversity hit so close to home for me. When I was first exposed to anime and manga, most caricatures of African Americans were very stereotypical. While there are some that slip through the cracks, we're seeing stories of BIPOC people in a better light. We also see more BIPOC people being inspired to join the manga/anime field; for example, D'Art Shtajio is the only African American-run studio in Japan. They have worked on multiple popular titles, such as *Attack on Titan*, *One Piece*, *Overlord*, and so on. We have Black authors, like Yase and Jacque Aye, who have published manga. It's so great to see this and appreciate the work that they do.

Q: Can you think of a particular time when a manga reader felt represented in manga, when they personally connected with the story or a character?
A: The BIPOC manga characters I found myself drawn to were Canary from *Hunter x Hunter* and Yoruichi Shihōin from *Bleach*. These titles came out when I was starting college (I'm 42 now and still love them). Just seeing badass BIPOC female characters being strong and handling their own was always refreshing. The same goes for *Michiko & Hatchin*, though this is not a manga. I absolutely love that anime series.

Satoko & Nada is another great manga series that promotes respect and cultural understanding, especially toward the Muslim community. Nada is from Saudi Arabia and Satoko is from Japan. Both are studying in America, and together they navigate through a culturally different world than they're used to.

While not a Black character, Shoko Komi from *Komi Can't Communicate* will always have a special place for me. I have an anxiety disorder and have a hard time trusting and connecting with people. Seeing Komi lets me know that I'm not alone and that it's okay to be different from what society expects me to be.

Q: What resources could librarians access to continue their professional development, to learn more about supporting the BIPOC community through manga?
- Anime News Network (animenewsnetwork.com)
- Black Girl Nerds (blackgirlnerds.com)
- Comic Book Resource (cbr.com)
- *Fantastic Frankey/Fanboy Fighter* (Podcaster and YouTuber)
- Good Comics for Kids (goodcomicsforkids.slj.com)
- *The Magical Girl's Guide to Life* by Jacque Aye
- Webtoons (webtoons.com)

Q: What manga titles would you recommend that have positive representations of the BIPOC community?

- *Adorned by Chi* by Jacque Aye, Magus Ato, and Tiana Mone'e (self published)
- *Beastars* by Paru Itagaki (VIZ Media)
- *Carole & Tuesday* by BONES, Shinichiro Watanabe, and Morito Yamataka (Yen Press)
- *Fire Force* by Atsushi Ohkubo (Kodansha)
- *Haikyu!!* by Haruichi Furudate (VIZ Media)
- *My Hero Academia* by Kohei Horikoshi (VIZ Media)
- *Princess Love Pon* by Shauna J. Grant (independently published on princesslovepon.com)
- *Satoko & Nada* by Yupechika (Seven Seas Entertainment)
- *Slam Dunk* by Takehiko Inoue (VIZ Media)
- *Soul Eater* by Atsushi Ohkubo (Yen Press)   /////

LATINX REPRESENTATION IN MANGA
An Interview with Karina Quilantan-Garza

Karina Quilantan-Garza (she/her), also known as Cue the Librarian, is an award-winning librarian, international and keynote presenter, and instructional designer from the Rio Grande Valley, Texas, who enjoys finding innovative ways to keep her students and staff engaged in the learning process. When she isn't saving the world one book at a time, she can be found connecting with educators on Twitter @cuethelibrarian.

Q: Why does positive representation in manga matter to our readers and to our communities?
Positive representation in manga matters because it validates communities and cultures that wouldn't otherwise be represented in mainstream media. Having representation in manga, and literature overall, validates and legitimizes our presence in traditionally Eurocentric spaces. It inspires others to create and be a part of narratives that tell our stories authentically. By enriching narratives available for leisure

and educational consumption, manga can reflect the sociocultural identities of readers and authors. Additionally, positive representation in manga allows us to compare and contrast our stories to find commonalities and embrace differences, thus inspiring new generations of storytellers to continue to create work for future readers who want to find themselves in the literature that they read. As an educator, I've found that one of the biggest obstacles is overcoming the barriers that adopted materials pose. I do this by finding supplemental materials that enhance the experience of our students of color and varying economic status. In their effort to break the cycles of institutionalized racism and bias that are often present in school-adopted materials, librarians can turn to manga, or graphic novels, to highlight stories that are representative of a spectrum of identities and populations and make reading for enjoyment accessible, relevant, and engaging for children and adults.

Q: How do manga creators illustrate positive representations of the Latinx community?
A: While manga has a long way to go in terms of representing the Latinx community accurately and authentically, the medium has begun to allow Latinx storytellers to control the narrative. This allows authors to represent their cultures in their true forms, instead of anglicized versions that are palatable to the white mainstream. There is a need for more representation rather than appropriation of stories. Manga can help us celebrate Latinx stories by featuring Latinx protagonists with major roles where people of color can be seen as the hero, and not just side characters or used as a plot device.

Q: Can you think of a particular time when a manga reader felt represented in manga, when they personally connected with the story or a character?
A: There is a lack of Latinx representation in manga, but many of my students who come to the United States from Mexico for school immerse themselves in manga because of their love of anime. This has created a culture of readers among my English language-learning population where they can share their love of the medium, art, authors, characters, and Japanese culture. Most of my library's circulation comes from the manga collection, and I think this is due to manga's inclusion of pictures

along with the text, which makes the students' language-acquisition journey accessible and engaging.

Q: What resources could librarians access to continue their professional development, to learn more about supporting the Latinx community through manga?
A: Much like the absence of Latinx stories in manga, there is also a lack of resources. It is important to consider that many of the resources that are available are self-made by those within the BIPOC community. Some tools and resources that have been extremely valuable in helping other librarians navigate this issue include the Manga in Libraries webinars, the No Flying No Tights website, subscriptions to library journals for reviews, and popular manga publishers. These resources can help librarians stay abreast of upcoming manga titles and releases. The better equipped and more immersed in the medium librarians are, the more efficient and effective their selection process for manga will be.

Q: What manga titles would you recommend that have positive representations of the Latinx community?
A: Unfortunately, there is an extreme lack of Latinx representation in manga. While there are many excellent manga titles that portray the BIPOC community positively, there is a need to include Latinx voices in the medium. Whether the future holds publications for Latinx communities is questionable; the medium would benefit from including manga that tell stories of Latinx folklore, the immigrant experience, and the sociopolitical struggles that Latinx countries face daily. Consequently, the absence of these stories will continue to alienate our voices and exacerbate a cycle of anti-inclusion.   /////

MANGA WITH POSITIVE REPRESENTATION

One organization leading the way in bringing more positive BIPOC and LGBTQ+ representation to manga is Saturday AM, founded by Frederick L. Jones. Saturday AM creates original English-language (OEL) manga. OEL manga is manga-inspired comics created outside of Japan, and originally published in English. OEL manga from Saturday AM is written and illustrated by diverse creators and feature diverse characters and stories. The stories are available digitally on their website, saturday-am.com, and at ComicsPlus, and in print at local bookstores.

Here are some Saturday AM titles to consider for your library collection:

- *Apple Black* by Odunze Oguguo
- *Clock Striker* by Frederick L. Jones and Issaka Galadima
- *Hammer* by JeyOdin
- *How to Draw Diverse Manga* by Saturday AM
- *Saigami* by Seni

For more information about positive representation in manga, check out the panel "Ushering in an Inclusive and Diverse Wave of Manga" with the founder and creators of Saturday AM. This panel was sponsored by Quarto Kids at the ALA's Annual Conference.[2]

EXPERT INTERVIEW TAKEAWAYS

What we as librarians can learn from all these expert interviews is that manga connects our global community and that people everywhere engage with this medium and seek stories that represent and reflect their lives. While diverse and inclusive representation in manga has improved over the years, there is still a long way to go in ensuring that all voices are positively represented and celebrated.

NOTES

1. American Library Association, "Equity, Diversity, and Inclusion," ala.org/advocacy/diversity.
2. Quarto Kids, "Ushering in an Inclusive and Diverse Wave of Manga Panel with Saturday AM," panel discussion at the ALA's 2022 Annual Conference (Washington, DC), video available on YouTube at youtube.com/watch?v=uGvXEjdiSCY.

SOCIAL-EMOTIONAL LEARNING AND MANGA

MANGA OFTEN REPRESENTS AND REFLECTS THE lives of teens and their lived personal experiences. Manga covers many topics that may not only give teens words to express what they are experiencing, but offer possible solutions for overcoming obstacles and becoming self-empowered. Through manga, teens can learn how to understand and reflect on their lives and the lives of others. Therefore, manga can be a support system for the social-emotional development of teens.

DEFINING SOCIAL-EMOTIONAL LEARNING

According to the Collaborative for Academic, Social, and Emotional Learning (CASEL), social-emotional learning (SEL) is "the process through which all young people and adults acquire and apply the knowledge, skills, and attitudes to develop healthy identities, manage emotions and achieve personal and collective goals, feel and show empathy for others, establish and maintain supportive relationships, and make responsible and caring decisions."[1]

Teens who learn these essential SEL skills can grow up to be incredibly successful in school, work, and life. Acquiring and reinforcing these SEL skills can also support teens with their ability to communicate, problem-solve, cope with challenges, and build tolerance. Teens who can show compassion and an awareness of the needs and perspectives of others are demonstrating strong SEL skills.

A school, classroom, or library that promotes SEL can have a positive impact on teens. These settings can allow teens to live, learn, and grow. When fostering environments that promote SEL, you are not just helping to develop the personal identity of teens, but preparing them for academic success, civic participation, and fulfilling lives.

According to CASEL, "most people agree that it is important for young people to have trusting relationships, a sense of purpose and belonging, and to learn and practice the skills needed to work toward their goals and contribute to their communities. That is why social and emotional learning (SEL) is important—because it can help create educational opportunities and environments that promote learning and practicing social, emotional, and academic skills, all of which are fundamental to healthy human development."[2]

CASEL'S SEL FRAMEWORK ADAPTED FOR LIBRARIES

CASEL's SEL framework is divided into five fundamentals: self-awareness, self-management, responsible decision-making, relationship skills, and social awareness. Each fundamental allows librarians to identify the main idea that should guide their pedagogy, their structures, and their community norms. Each fundamental is also connected to skills that should be reinforced through positive, safe, and inclusive learning opportunities for teens.

When it comes to library instruction, programs, and collections, consider which SEL skills you want to reinforce. The goal is to provide teens with the chance to learn, demonstrate, and master these SEL skills. This growth can be achieved independently or collectively within a collaborative learning environment.

CASEL'S FIVE FUNDAMENTALS OF SEL

Whatever a teen's personal experience and cultural background may be, by reinforcing CASEL's five fundamentals of SEL, teens will be able to acquire and develop the following skills during authentic and reflective learning experiences in the library.

1. **Self-Awareness:** "The abilities to understand one's own emotions, thoughts, and values and how they influence behavior across contexts."[3]

   SEL Skills: Teens will be able to identify and process their emotions and reflect on their own strengths and identities. Skills include being able to:
     - Integrate personal and social identities
     - Identify personal, cultural, and linguistic assets

- Identify one's emotions
- Demonstrate honesty and integrity
- Link feelings, values, and thoughts
- Examine prejudices and biases
- Experience self-efficacy
- Have a growth mindset
- Develop interests and a sense of purpose[4]

2. **Self-Management:** "The abilities to manage one's emotions, thoughts, and behaviors effectively in different situations and to achieve goals and aspirations."[5]

SEL *Skills:* Teens will be able to set goals, manage stress, and demonstrate resilience. Skills include being able to:
- Manage one's emotions
- Identify and use stress-management strategies
- Exhibit self-discipline and self-motivation
- Set personal and collective goals
- Use planning and organizational skills
- Show the courage to take initiative
- Demonstrate personal and collective agency[6]

3. **Social Awareness:** "The abilities to understand the perspectives of and empathize with others, including those from diverse backgrounds, cultures, and contexts."[7]

SEL *Skills:* Teens will be able to empathize and take into account the perspectives of other people from similar and different backgrounds. Skills include being able to:
- Take others' perspectives
- Recognize strengths in others
- Demonstrate empathy and compassion
- Show concern for the feelings of others
- Understand and express gratitude
- Identify diverse social norms, including unjust ones
- Recognize situational demands and opportunities
- Understand the influences of organizations/systems on behavior
- Demonstrate personal and collective agency[8]

4. **Relationship Skills:** "The abilities to establish and maintain healthy and supportive relationships and to effectively navigate settings with diverse individuals and groups."[9]

   SEL Skills: Teens will be able to establish and maintain healthy relationships and collaboratively find solutions to challenges. Skills include being able to:
   - Communicate effectively
   - Develop positive relationships
   - Demonstrate cultural competency
   - Practice teamwork and collaborative problem-solving
   - Resolve conflicts constructively
   - Resist negative social pressure
   - Show leadership in groups
   - Seek or offer support and help when needed
   - Stand up for the rights of others[10]

5. **Responsible Decision-Making:** "The abilities to make caring and constructive choices about personal behavior and social interactions across diverse situations."[11]

   SEL Skills: Teens will be able to analyze situations, solve problems, and make decisions that promote collective well-being. Skills include being able to:
   - Demonstrate curiosity and open-mindedness
   - Identify solutions for personal and social problems
   - Learn to make a reasoned judgment after analyzing information, data, and facts
   - Anticipate and evaluate the consequences of one's actions
   - Recognize how critical thinking skills are useful both inside and outside of the library
   - Reflect on one's role to promote personal, family, and community well-being
   - Evaluate personal, interpersonal, community, and institutional impacts[12]

READING MANGA SUPPORTS SEL

Reading manga can support teens in a variety of ways, including helping them to understand multiple perspectives, develop empathy and compassion, and personally connect with others' experiences. Reading manga helps teens to explore identities, improve their emotional intelligence, and develop social and emotional well-being. Reading manga can also help to reduce stress and anxiety and provide teens with the opportunity to momentarily escape the pressures of life.

Libraries need to ensure that they have books in their collections that engage teens in SEL. By establishing a manga collection that aligns with CASEL's five fundamentals of SEL, you can help to support the social-emotional development of teens. But not all manga titles have to connect with all five of the fundamentals. You can focus on identifying and exploring one fundamental or on multiple fundamentals of SEL, or you can choose to focus on one or more skills within a fundamental.

MANGA TITLES THAT CONNECT TO SEL

Here are some manga titles to consider when exploring CASEL's five fundamentals of SEL.

Self-Awareness
- *Beastars* by Paru Itagaki (VIZ Media)
- *Boys Run the Riot* by Keito Gaku (Kodansha)
- *Wandance* by Coffee (Kodansha)

Self-Management
- *Demon Slayer* by Koyoharu Gotouge (VIZ Media)
- *Haikyu!!* by Haruichi Furudate (VIZ Media)
- *The Promised Neverland*, story by Kaiu Shirai, art by Posuka Demizu (VIZ Media)

Social Awareness
- *I Think Our Son Is Gay* by Okura (Square Enix)
- *A Silent Voice* by Yoshitoki Oima (Kodansha)
- *Yuzu the Pet Vet* by Mingo Ito (Kodansha)

Relationship Skills
- *The Golden Sheep* by Kaori Ozaki (Kodansha)
- *Komi Can't Communicate* by Tomohito Oda (VIZ Media)
- *Love in Focus* by Yoko Nogiri (Kodansha)

Responsible Decision-Making
- *I Want to Be a Wall* by Honami Shirono (Yen Press)
- *Our Dreams at Dusk* by Yuhki Kamatani (Seven Seas Entertainment)
- *Perfect World* by Rie Aruga (Kodansha)

MANGA AND EMOTIONAL INTELLIGENCE

Manga is an emotional storytelling format, as it often connects with a teen's core emotions. This connection gives readers an opportunity to recognize and reflect on these emotions. Aside from the characters in manga being visually expressive with their emotions, the story itself often involves characters facing moments of great emotion, and openly expressing these emotions through their thoughts and/or actions.

Being able to identify one's emotions and the emotions of others, as well as knowing how to monitor and regulate one's emotions and the emotions of others, is a sure sign of emotional intelligence. Emotional intelligence is connected to SEL but is not a skill that every teen innately has. But emotional intelligence can develop through learning opportunities that encourage thoughtful discussion and reflection regarding the emotions of the characters and the readers.

The Feelings Wheel

The Feelings Wheel is a visual tool that is used to help recognize and communicate emotions.[13] The Feelings Wheel can also help teens to identify the emotions of characters in manga. While there are a vast range of human emotions, and we might only have words for some of them, the opportunity to reflect on a character's emotions can increase the emotional intelligence of teens. Teens can use the Feelings Wheel to not only discuss what emotions that character is feeling or expressing, but reflect on where these emotions stem from and how such emotions might be universally shared with teens despite their differing personal experiences and background.

There are six core emotions at the center of the Feelings Wheel: sad, mad, scared, joyful, powerful, and peaceful. (See figure 4.1.) Once the core emotion is identified, then there are two outer circles of secondary emotions that are more complex and often more difficult to identify. Teens can identify a core emotion on the Feelings Wheel and then move to the companion outer circles to identify more specific emotions that connect to the situation.

FIGURE 4.1 | The Feelings Wheel

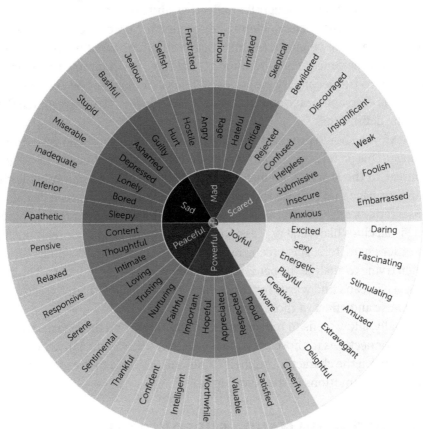

Source: Image licensed with a CC BY-SA 4.0 license (https://creativecommons.org/licenses/by-sa/4.0) via Wikimedia Commons, https://commons.wikimedia.org/wiki/File:The_Feeling_Wheel.png; the figure has been adapted to black and white.

The Feelings Wheel can be used for personal reflection to reflect on one's own mental health. Or the wheel can be used to reflect on manga and provide words for teens to understand and empathize with the emotional expressions of the characters. When teens can identify emotions more accurately, they can learn how to respond to and reflect on those emotions more effectively.

USING THE FEELINGS WHEEL TO DISCUSS MANGA

When first introducing the Feelings Wheel to teens, ensure that the learning environment for this discussion is a safe space. Then collaboratively as a group, establish norms for a respectful discussion. Aim to facilitate a dialogue between teens that is thoughtful, reflective, and honest.

First, work with teens to identify and define the six core emotions. What do teens think of when they think of each emotion? What words, phrases, ideas, or experiences come to mind? Once the core emotions are defined, move on to the secondary emotions. While there may not be enough time to define each emotion, you can certainly provide teens with a resource that has the definitions.

Next, you should provide teens with a single panel or a single page from a manga. This panel or page can be provided alongside the book blurb to give context to the story. Or to make it more challenging, you can provide the panel or page and remove the text. The goal is to allow the teens to make observations and assumptions about the emotions of the characters based on visual clues like facial expressions, body language, and their relationship to other characters. Have teens use the emotions from the Feelings Wheel when trying to analyze the panel or page and express their thoughts. The goal is to have teens find words for those emotions and allow them to recognize the cause and effect of those emotions.

Finally, allow teens to reflect on those emotions. Can they make any personal connections to those emotions? Can they identify the impact of those emotions on the character and their community? Would they express similar or different emotions in the given situation?

REFLECTING ON MANGA SUPPORTS SEL

If you are interested in fostering an SEL environment in your library, developing emotional intelligence is one of the keys to a teen's success. Providing teens with the tools and skills to support them is essential as they go through one of the most developmentally difficult periods of their lives.

To contribute to a teen's social-emotional development, facilitate conversations about manga with the opportunity to reflect on all five of CASEL's fundamentals of SEL. You can engage teens in thoughtful reflections and discussions about what they have read and what they have learned through manga. These thoughtful reflections and discussions can deepen a teen's reading and learning experiences. These conversations can be informal and happen with teens independently, or they can take place formally in a book club so that teens can better understand themselves and others. The goal of these reflections and discussions is to help create a safe space for teens and build a bond within the library community.

MANGA REFLECTION AND DISCUSSION PROMPTS

Question Prompts That Support Self-Awareness and Self-Management

Identify and Respond to Emotions

- What are some things that made the character feel . . . Mad? Sad? Happy?
- What strategies did the character use to help cope with these difficult emotions?
- How did these emotions impact the character's actions?
- How did the character communicate their emotions?
- Was there a time when the character needed help? How was this resolved?
- What emotions is the character good at expressing?
- What strategies is the character using to express their emotions?
- How does the character contribute to their community?
- Who in the community can the character go to for help?
- What internal qualities or external supports have helped the character accept new challenges and adjust to change?

Question Prompts That Support Social Awareness and Relationship Skills

Recognize the Feelings and Perspectives of Others

- How has the character demonstrated the ability to adopt the perspectives of others?
- How would you describe the character's personal identity? How is it similar or different than that of the people around them?
- What are some ways that the character shows concern for their friends or family?
- What are some ways that the character shows leadership skills?
- What communication strengths and challenges does the character demonstrate?
- When has the character struggled? What did the character learn about themselves?
- How does the character demonstrate an ability to prevent, manage, and resolve interpersonal conflicts in constructive ways?

Question Prompts That Support Responsible Decision-Making

Consider Ethical, Safety, and Societal Factors in Making Decisions

- What kinds of things did the character think about when making a decision?
- How have the character's choices impacted the people and world around them?
- What decisions has the character made that were strongly guided by their ethics?
- What is a positive decision that the character made? How did they make their choice?
- How would you have handled a situation differently than the character? What would have happened if that decision had been made instead?
- What are some ways that the character has helped others?
- Who are some people that make a difference in the character's life?

Source: Adapted from CASEL, "SEL Reflection Prompts," 2020, https://casel.s3.us-east-2.amazonaws.com/SEL-Reflection-Prompts.pdf.

ANALYZING MANGA FOR SEL

Providing teens with a chance to discuss manga in a group will allow them to see how other people react to the story, to hear other perspectives, and to understand other people by building empathy. When having community conversations about manga and SEL, provide teens with these two critical lenses to frame the discussion:

1. How does the *mangaka* support the character's social-emotional development?
2. How does the *manga* support the reader's social-emotional development?

These critical lenses will help to not only frame the reading experience, but the teens' reflections.

SEL AND *KOMI CAN'T COMMUNICATE*

An example of a manga that can be read and analyzed for CASEL's five fundamentals of SEL is *Komi Can't Communicate*, vol. 1, by Tomohito Oda. Komi has extreme social anxiety, and as a result she struggles with the ability to communicate effectively with her peers. At the start of the new school year, Komi meets classmate Tadano, who notices that Komi has difficulty communicating. One day in the classroom, Komi and Tadano start communicating via the chalkboard, and it is here that Komi realizes that she wants to make 100 new friends. This growth mindset is what allows teens to explore Komi's social-emotional development.

In the first few chapters of *Komi Can't Communicate*, three fundamentals of SEL are demonstrated: self-management, self-awareness, and relationships skills. These three fundamentals are expressed consistently throughout the manga. They relate directly to the intention of the *mangaka* to explore the challenges that Komi faces, to see the impact of having a supportive friendship, and to show her growth when she risks changing for the better.

As teens read, they can use a graphic organizer to help analyze the manga for CASEL's five fundamentals of SEL. Sections of the graphic organizer can include the fundamentals and the skill(s) of SEL, the evidence collected from the manga, and the page numbers of that evidence. While completing the SEL graphic organizer, teens can also consider the following questions: What factors allow Komi to grow? What factors challenge Komi, force her to make a choice, take a stand, or take a chance? What factors allow Komi to demonstrate the fundamentals of SEL? This graphic organizer will help students to participate in a collaborative discussion about the factors that support or challenge Komi's social-emotional development.

TEEN THOUGHTS ON MANGA AND SEL

After having taught CASEL's five fundamentals of SEL, and having read and analyzed a few manga titles with teens in my library, I engaged teens in a meaningful conversation about manga and SEL. We specifically focused on the people, the environment, and the events that could either support or prevent a character's social-emotional development in manga. We also spoke about how SEL opportunities could be a catalyst for the social-emotional development of teens. After this reflection, I asked them the following question: "Do you think manga can support the social-emotional development of teens?" I then documented their responses.

- "I think that manga can support the social-emotional development of teens. While manga is more on the side of being an animated form of reading, including more visuals than words, it demonstrates the true character development that all ages can clearly see. Social-emotional development is more comprehended through works of art and actual visuals, since it is commonly found that most learners are visual learners. Personally, manga for me has shaped how I come across a conflict within friendships, relationships, or even myself. I try not to embody but incorporate the traits that characters that I feel connect to me show. Overall, manga not only is there for entertainment but also helps society see their own character development through the eyes, ears, and thoughts of what characters demonstrate inside of their own worlds."
- "I strongly believe manga can support the social-emotional development of teens, which is why I enjoy manga so much in the first place. The way manga connects with the reader through experiences that are more complex or niche, makes it easier for the reader to relate to what the main character is experiencing on a much more personal level, which is why manga does such a good job at supporting the social-emotional development of their readers."

- "Yes, because with the added visual component in manga, it's easier for readers to identify emotion and the social context of that emotion."
- "Yes, I compared myself to some characters and connected to some emotions I didn't even realize I was feeling."
- "I do think manga can support the social-emotional development of teens because the way manga is written allows readers to relate to and feel empathy for the characters. There are speech bubbles and sound effects in manga that allow readers to hear and feel the same things as characters."
- "Yes, for many reasons. When I first began to learn about SEL, I found it challenging to apply it to the manga we read, and especially outside of class. As the class went on, I slowly got the hang of it and I found that I can apply SEL anywhere I go, from other books and movies to my own thoughts and emotions."
- "I believe it can because it introduces a new type of media from a different country with different ideals and taboos, so it forces the reader to try and understand the world from a different view and different cultures to them. The art style can also heavily impact how someone can see SEL; it lets the reader see how [the characters] react and not just read it in words."
- "SEL allowed me to understand myself by resonating with the characters we read in the manga. I was able to understand my emotions and my actions, and I used it to understand those around me who were struggling or stressed. I think those who are struggling with their emotions or those that have a lot going on in their lives will benefit."
- "Yes, because teens might relate to problems the main character is facing and can identify with them easily."
- "Yes, the way we see the characters grow and develop in the manga we read, can allow us to grow and develop and implement these skills in real life."
- "Manga can support the social-emotional development of teens because a lot of people can connect to the stories being told about the characters and this may reflect on the reader's own experiences."
- "Manga has helped me with my own social-emotional learning because it is okay to have conflict within our lives, whether that be relationships or personal. But the manga helped me understand that everything will work out no matter the circumstance, with the help of friends, family, and our own personal growth."

According to these readers, manga can support the social-emotional development of teens. Their argument states that teens can find comfort in the stories. They can see their personal experiences reflected at them through manga, which brings validity to their lived experiences. Teens are exposed to different perspectives, which can allow them to become more empathetic towards one another. Through manga, teens can learn life lessons and find the motivation to enact change in their lives, seeing that it is possible. If teens have similar issues, they can learn from the characters' emotions and experiences and apply what they learn to their own lives to grow and support their social-emotional development. Providing teens with a chance to not only reflect on the social-emotional development of the characters within manga, but to reflect on the impact that this could have on teens, will absolutely help to foster their social-emotional development.

NOTES

1. "Fundamentals of SEL," CASEL, https://casel.org/fundamentals-of-sel/.
2. "How Does SEL Support Educational Equity and Excellence?" CASEL, https://casel.org/fundamentals-of-sel/how-does-sel-support-educational -equity-and-excellence/.
3. "CASEL's SEL Framework," CASEL, 2020, https://casel.org/casel-sel-frame-work-11-2020/?view=true.
4. "CASEL's SEL Framework."
5. "CASEL's SEL Framework."
6. "CASEL's SEL Framework."
7. "CASEL's SEL Framework."
8. "CASEL's SEL Framework."
9. "CASEL's SEL Framework."
10. "CASEL's SEL Framework."
11. "CASEL's SEL Framework."
12. "CASEL's SEL Framework."
13. Gloria Willcox, "The Feeling Wheel," *Transactional Analysis Journal* 12, no. 4 (1982): 274–76, doi: 10.1177/036215378201200411.

MANGA PROGRAMMING

IN MANY WAYS, MANGA IS A COMMON LANGUAGE that unites teens from all different backgrounds. Manga is also a means for socialization because it can provide opportunities for teens to have positive interactions with their peers, their found family. Teens also need safe spaces, where they can explore their interests, engage in activities that meet their needs, and express themselves freely. So, when designing library programs, consider how to use manga to foster those safe spaces and build a sense of community for your teens.

MANGA CULTURE AND COMMUNITY

When it comes to manga programs, you can engage teens through manga book clubs, anime watch parties, teen-led workshops, special events, and more. These opportunities help to build a culture and community within the library, provide opportunities for collaboration with peers and professionals, and engage teens in authentic learning experiences.

There are a variety of ways to bring manga programs to your library, such as through a lunch club or an after-school club that meets daily, weekly, or monthly. This depends on the availability of the library space, the availability of the librarian facilitating the programs, and the needs of the teens participating in the programs.

MANGA PROGRAMS' LEARNING OBJECTIVES

In my school library, I have hosted a variety of different manga programs that range from a 40-minute lunch club to a 3-hour-a-week after-school club, to daily, monthly, and annual events. All these programs were driven by the needs and interests of the teens in my school. But before I designed these manga programs for the library, I considered what learning objectives I wanted the programs to meet. Here are some of the learning objectives that I have considered for manga programs in my library.

The manga program will . . .

- Develop a culture of reading and increase circulation
- Provide engaging, authentic, and hands-on learning experiences

The teens participating will . . .

- Build skills that will increase their academic achievement at school, such as reading, visual literacy, cultural literacy, collaboration, leadership, and presentation skills
- Engage in a community of shared interests and mutual respect

MANGA PROGRAMS FOR LIBRARIES

The following manga programs are all ones that I have hosted in my school library. These programs can be adapted to meet any age, any budget, and any timeline.

Hosting a Forty-Minute Manga Club

When I started working at my school library, middle school students advocated for a Manga Club, something that the school community had not yet offered. I took them up on this opportunity because of their passion and my professional interest in learning more about manga. So I began to host the Manga Club throughout the school year, once a week, during lunch. During these forty minutes students read and discussed manga, provided their peers with manga suggestions for reading, watched and discussed anime, and created and critiqued original stories and artwork to be hung in the library's Artist Alley. The following are some activities that you can apply to your Manga Club.

Activity One: Manga Interest Survey

Start your Manga Club with a Manga Interest Survey that allows all teens to get a sense of the community. Ask them a variety of questions that will allow them to express their ideas and interests and connect to those of their peers.

Manga Interest Survey: Questions about Manga

- Why do you like reading manga?
- How often do you read manga?
- What is your favorite manga series?
- What is your favorite manga genre?
- What manga are you currently reading?
- Do you have a favorite manga character?
- What is your least favorite manga?
- What is most important in manga, the story or the art?
- Have you ever tried to get other teens interested in manga?

Manga Interest Survey: Questions about Anime

- Why do you like watching anime?
- How often do you watch anime?
- What is your favorite anime?
- What is your favorite anime genre?
- What anime are you currently watching?
- What is your least favorite anime?
- What anime do you want to watch that you have not yet watched?
- Have you ever tried to get other teens interested in anime?

Activity Two: Manga Book Club

Hosting a Manga Book Club will allow teens to have a shared reading experience with their peers, and it can also help to increase book circulation and community engagement. You can start a Manga Book Club following these five steps.

Step One: Planning the Manga Book Club

Determine the audience for the Manga Book Club. Will it serve a middle school or high school population? Once the audience is determined, consider the goals of the Manga Book Club. What are the learning objectives for teens?

Step Two: Advertising the Manga Book Club

Once you determine the availability of the library, advertise the date, time, and location of the first meeting of the Manga Book Club.

Step Three: Hosting the Manga Book Club

At the first meeting, give teens the chance to learn about the other members of the Manga Book Club. Then, allow teens to discuss and make decisions about the Manga Book Club experience, including what type of manga to read, the schedule and format of the meetings, and any other ideas that they may have.

Step Four: Manga Book Club Selections

Provide teens with some criteria in advance of selecting possible titles for the Manga Book Club. Some criteria to consider may include single volume vs. multiple volumes, readership and genres, and digital vs. print. Then have teens work in small groups to research and propose some titles to the club, and then vote for the final selections.

Things to consider: How will you acquire copies of the manga titles that the teens select? Will teens be required to purchase their own copies? Or will the library provide the copies? Will these copies be print or digital? Will a budget or fundraising be required?

Step Five: Reading and Discussing Manga

After the titles have been selected, work with teens to determine the norms of the Manga Book Club. What are the expectations for reading? What ideas or questions should teens consider while reading? How will teens prepare for discussing the manga? What norms should be followed when sharing thoughts and opinions?

Things to consider: What questions will you use to moderate discussions about the manga? Will you prepare these questions in advance? Or will teens be required to develop these questions? If teens are required to moderate discussions, provide a learning opportunity to teach teens how to do so successfully.

If you need additional support, check out the *Manga Book Club Handbook* created by the Comic Book Legal Defense Fund and VIZ Media. This handbook provides information on getting a book club started, selecting books, reading them, discussing them, and more.

Some ways you can enhance the Manga Book Club is by considering additional activities such as creating a manga awards list, hosting a manga Battle of the Books, offering a manga reading challenge with prizes, creating a manga podcast, or manga social media videos.

Activity Three: Anime Club

Anime is Japanese animation that has a variety of art styles and genres, presented in the form of film and television series. Anime can be watched on streaming services such as Hulu, Netflix, and Crunchyroll. Manga is often adapted from anime series, and vice versa. Examples of anime series are *Spy x Family*, *Kaguya-Sama: Love Is War*, and *Demon Slayer*.

Hosting an Anime Club is another opportunity to foster a shared learning experience for teens. Watching anime is often a gateway for teens to begin reading manga, so celebrating anime in your library can help to inspire new manga readers. If you are not too familiar with anime, you can easily designate teen leaders to facilitate the Anime Club.

Of course, like hosting a Manga Book Club, you would want to start by creating a plan and advertising the Anime Club. At the first meeting, discuss with teens the norms and expectations of the club, which includes selecting, viewing, and discussing anime. Just like manga, the anime should also be vetted in advance to ensure that it meets the needs and interests of your community.

Things to consider: How will teens watch anime in the library? Does the library already have anime in the collection? Do teens have anime in their personal collections? Does the library have access to anime streaming services? Or does the library block these streaming services? Does the library need permission to stream anime?

You should also consider providing teens with comfortable seating and snacks while they watch and discuss anime. Some discussion questions may include:

- What did you like best/least about the anime?
- In what ways were you able to connect to the anime?
- What question(s) would you ask the creator(s) of the anime?
- How does the anime compare to the manga?

Some ways you can enhance the Anime Club is by considering additional activities such as creating a "Top Ten" anime list, hosting an anime drawing workshop or contest, reading manga, playing anime-themed games and trivia, or learning the Japanese language.

Hosting a Three-Hour Japanese Culture & Manga Club

At my school, I noticed that the middle school students in the Manga Club were eager to learn more about Japanese culture. At the same time, the high school students were eager to start their own Manga Club. With limited time and limited resources, I went to my administration and advocated for the opportunity to host a Japanese Culture & Manga Club, an after-school program that would allow me to combine both middle school and high school students.

The Japanese Culture & Manga Club was approved and was hosted in the library, after school, for three hours per week. During this time, students continued to read and discuss manga, watch and discuss anime, and create and critique artwork. But the additional bonus was that now students throughout grades 6–12 were able to work and learn together and celebrate their passion and interest in Japanese culture and manga. The high school students became role models for the middle school students. They provided extra support during learning experiences, provided them with book recommendations, and engaged in enthusiastic conversations about their common interests.

Now that the Japanese Culture & Manga Club was established, the next step was figuring out how to provide students with programs that included authentic learning experiences. What did students want to learn? What did they already know? How was I going to provide them with high-quality programming? How would these additional learning experiences enhance their knowledge of manga and anime? I decided to research local community organizations that might be able to visit my school and provide students with authentic Japanese culture programs.

Collaborating with Resobox

When researching community organizations, I found Resobox, a Japanese cultural center in Queens, New York City. Resobox offers classes and events, workshops, and exhibits that allow members of the community to celebrate

Japanese culture. I decided to reach out to the owner of Resobox, and in response, they offered to come to my school library to provide eight weeks of Japanese culture programs, hosted by Japanese educators and artists—but at a cost of $2,000. Now my problem was funding, the problem being that I had none. So I did research on how I could acquire funding to host these programs. That is when I discovered AASL's Inspire Special Event Grant.

I applied for and was lucky enough to receive the Inspire Special Event Grant. This grant provided me with the funds needed to cover the eight weeks of Japanese culture programs for students in the Japanese Culture & Manga Club. The programs consisted of manga drawing and animation, Japanese ink painting and calligraphy, Japanese language, and Japanese cooking and sushi-making workshops. This opportunity was completely transformative for the students.

Students were able to learn how to create their own *yonkoma* manga stories, while also learning about storyboarding and illustration. They learned about *sumi-e*, Japanese ink-and-brush painting and calligraphy. Here they also learned how to write in Kanji, and they listened to traditional Japanese music. During the Japanese language workshops, students learned how to greet each other, share personal facts about themselves like their name and age, and engage in simple conversation with peers. The bonus was the sushi-making workshop. Students were able to use vegetable-dyed rice to craft sushi into the shape of Totoro from *My Neighbor Totoro*.

Community Organizations

Aside from Resobox, there may be other Japanese culture centers across the country that would like the opportunity to provide authentic learning experiences for teens. But if it is not possible to bring an organization like Resobox into your library, consider connecting with other community organizations and experts. Consider connecting with a public library, a school library, a local bookstore, or a local comics shop. It is quite possible that you could collaborate with them for programming and share funding. You could also consider connecting with a local community member, a friend or parent with a special skill or talent, or a professor at a local college with expert knowledge. These visits can be done in-person or virtually, possibly at minimal cost or for free. You could also collaborate with other clubs and programs in your school or library. Consider working with the Gender

Sexuality Alliance, a film club, or a teen leadership group. Or have confidence in your library programming skills and facilitate Japanese culture programs with the support of the teens in your club.

Japanese Culture Programs

Hosting Japanese culture programs in the library is an opportunity for you to bring cultural awareness to teens, to build their understanding of another culture or to deepen their appreciation of their own culture. Remember to remain culturally sensitive when planning Japanese culture programs in the library, so as not to create or perpetuate stereotypes; instead, use this as an opportunity for teens to learn about and celebrate the history, culture, and traditions of Japan.

To bring Japanese culture learning experiences to your library, consider facilitating some of the following programs and adding some of the following books from Tuttle Publishing to your collection. (Tuttle Publishing is an international publisher that focuses on Japanese, Chinese, and Southeast Asian cultures.)

To bring the appreciation of Japanese cuisine and cooking into your library, use cookbooks to try some Japanese recipes and consider the following programs.

Host an event where teens can learn about and make ramen. Questions for exploring ramen can include: Why is ramen significant to Japanese cuisine? How do you make ramen? What meats, veggies, broths, and toppings can be added to ramen? Books for exploring ramen include *The Ultimate Japanese Noodles* by Masahiro Kasahara and *Japan Eats!* by Betty Reynolds.

Host an event where teens can learn about and create bento boxes. Questions for exploring bento boxes can include: What is the history of bento boxes in Japan? What types of food can be found in a bento box? How can you make the food items in a bento box visually appealing? Books for exploring bento boxes include *Fresh Bento* by Wendy Thorpe Copley and *Ultimate Bento* by Maki Ogawa and Marc Matsumoto. Digital bento boxes can also be made with a tool like Canva.

To bring the appreciation of Japanese arts into your library, use some art books to help teens draw and craft. Books on Japanese drawing and crafting include *Drawing Basic Manga Characters*, *Fun and Easy Origami Animals*, *Shodo: The Quiet Art of Japanese Zen Calligraphy*, *A Beginner's Guide to Sumi-e*,

Adorable Amigurumi—Cute and Quirky Crochet Critters, and *A Beginner's Guide to Quilling Paper Flowers*. Some of these activities may require funding for materials.

To bring still more Japanese culture into your library, explore some books about holidays and festivals, gaming and cosplay, and more. Books on Japanese culture can include *Introduction to Japanese Culture, All About Japan, Tokyo Geek's Guide*, and *Cool Guide Japan*.

Japanese Culture & Manga Club Field Trips

Another way to provide teens with authentic and engaging learning experiences is to leave the library and go out into the community to explore. You can take teens to see an anime film at a movie theater, shop at a Japanese bookstore or clothing store, visit a Japanese art exhibit or museum, eat at a Japanese market or restaurant, and more.

At my school, I met with my administration and received approval to begin taking the students of the Japanese Culture & Manga Club on field trips. Our first field trip was to Kinokuniya, a Japanese bookstore and cafe in Manhattan, New York City. Kinokuniya has multiple locations across the country, but any local comics shop or bookstore that sells manga will provide a similar experience. At Kinokuniya, students were able to explore and purchase manga, chat with booksellers, and hang out in the cafe and sip some bubble tea. Since then I have taken students on multiple trips to Kinokuniya, while also adding visits to Sunrise Mart, MUJI, and other Japanese-owned businesses.

Manga and Anime Conventions

A few years ago, I began working with ReedPop, the organization that hosts New York Comic Con. This partnership initially started as a way for me to support their professional development programs for librarians. But it has since developed to allow me to bring students to New York Comic Con annually with complimentary passes. At New York Comic Con, students can attend panel discussions, visit publishers' booths, and surround themselves with people who share similar interests. Many students would not have the opportunity to attend New York Comic Con on their own or with their families, so for many this experience has been life changing. I recently established a partnership with LeftField Media, the organization that runs Anime NYC, where I have also had the opportunity to bring students to the event annually with complimentary passes. Identify any pop culture conventions that are held within your community and see if you can establish a relationship that would allow you to bring teens to the event with discounted or complimentary passes.

International Travel to Japan

For the students in my Japanese Culture & Manga Club, our field trips around New York City only got them more interested in Japanese culture. So I decided to take our club to the next level and plan an international trip to Japan. The trip is scheduled for spring 2023 with EF Educational Tours so that students can authentically experience Japanese culture firsthand. The nine-day trip to Japan offered by EF includes airflight, housing, tours, food, and transportation. The cities we will visit include Tokyo, Hakone, Kyoto, and Osaka. Major attractions will include the Asakusa Kannon Temple, the Great Buddha of Kamakura, and a guided tour of Nara. To learn more about the trip, check out the trip on the EF Educational Tours website.

The Library Crew

I also host a program called Library Crew, which consists of a group of student volunteers. These volunteers help in the library by completing tasks ranging from creating bulletin boards and book displays to shelving and selecting books, hosting events, and helping their peers find books. As librarians, we know that teens can assume a variety of leadership roles within the library. These leadership roles can help teens to set goals, organize plans, and execute ideas required to achieve the goals. Students in the Library Crew assume leadership roles that allow them to collaborate with peers, library workers, and community members. The students enhance their presentation and speaking skills; develop a deeper understanding of library structures and programs; learn to think critically and problem-solve; and make connections to the real world, their personal lives, and the interests of their peers. Consider starting a Library Crew for all the wonderful benefits that it will have for teens in your community.

Manga Advisory Department

The Library Crew is a general group of student volunteers who are interested in the overall mission and goals of the library. But I realized that we needed a branch of the Library Crew to focus specifically on manga. As a result, I decided to start a high school program called the Manga Advisory Department. This program provides students who are super invested in Japanese culture and manga an opportunity to focus on their main interests. The program also gives students a voice in the library regarding the manga collection and programs. The Manga Advisory Department is responsible for building and maintaining the manga collection. They also help to plan and host manga programs and events that engage the community.

There are five roles in the Manga Advisory Department: president, secretary, reviewers, collection developers, and event coordinators. Each role has specific responsibilities: the president plans all the meetings, identifies and sets the goals, and delegates and monitors tasks. The secretary supports the president at all meetings, takes meeting notes, shares any communications with members or peers, and maintains the calendar. The reviewers write manga book reviews, provide manga suggestions for peers, and market and promote the manga collection through posters and signage. The collection developers research and inform the librarian about what manga to purchase for the library; they also identify any missing books, or series that need to be continued, as well as research and inform the librarian of what manga to purchase for the library. The event coordinators help to plan and host manga programs and events, as well as the library's annual Comic Con. The Manga Advisory Department has become an essential branch of the Library Crew.

Library Comic Con

I started hosting a library Comic Con during my first year at my school. Comic Con is a two-day event, hosted in the school library, that is open to all students grades 6–12. Since the Library Crew and the Manga Advisory Department are involved, they design and lead most of the events and programs. Students are often very excited about being leaders in their own learning, so they become incredibly invested. While the themes shift every year based on what is trending in pop culture, there is consistently programming around manga and anime. Day one is usually a series of stations, so that students can come into the library and explore a variety of activities. Day two is usually structured activities, often run by the Library Crew and the Manga Advisory Department.

Planning a Library Comic Con

When preparing for Comic Con, I meet with the Library Crew and the Manga Advisory Department about two months in advance. We discuss our vision, our program goals, and of course the logistics for hosting this event. When we set goals, we need to make sure that everything is achievable, realistic, and manageable. We ask ourselves: What stations will we host? What structured activities will we host? Once we know what programs we are hosting, we can decide what materials we will need. Then we divide and conquer; we plan the tasks for the students and the librarian to accomplish. After that, we create a schedule with deadlines. Over the course of the two months before the event, I often check in with the students to make sure that everyone is on track. Now that we have our goals set, our tasks determined, and our schedule outlined, we need to make a map of how the library will need to be set up on each day of the event.

Mapping Comic Con Activities

Day one of Comic Con could consist of 5–6 station activities that will require groups of tables and chairs, the library couches, the laptops, the Promethean board, and more. Day one's station activities could include, but are not limited to: anime watch parties, a photo booth with cardboard cutouts or a green screen, a reading corner with a "Best Manga" poll, technology apps or websites for making an avatar or creating a comic, and craft kits for buttons, keychains, bookmarks, coloring, drawing, and more.

Day two's structured activities vary, and therefore the library space must be shifted to meet the specific needs. Day two's structured activities could include but are not limited to: hosting a pop culture panel, guided workshops, trivia competitions, author and illustrator visits, gaming tournaments, and more. If we are hosting a trivia competition, the library could stay the same, with the tables and chairs. If we are hosting a gaming tournament, we need to move out all the tables, acquire more chairs, and set up multiple projectors and screens around the library. The map of the library's setup each day is extremely important and useful for the students who will be helping before and during the event.

Comic Con Budget

I do not have a budget for Comic Con, but I have written a DonorsChoose every year that has consistently been fulfilled. (DonorsChoose is an online charity that enables people to donate directly to public school classroom projects.) I also always provide snacks during Comic Con, as well as prizes for the winners of the various contests and competitions. Snacks I usually purchase, but prizes have included manga, Funko Pops, keychains, and other goodies that I usually get for free while attending New York Comic Con and Anime NYC. I have also reached out to VIZ Media in the past, and they have provided a lot of prizes for Comic Con. If you host a club or convention in your library, you can request promotional items and prizes from VIZ Media by just filling out this form: viz.com/company/contact_donation_form.

Moderating a Pop Culture Panel

Hosting a pop culture panel in the library is a great way to allow teens to take ownership of their learning experiences. This teen panel could happen as a part of a Manga Club or a library Comic Con, or it can happen as a special event at any point in the year. The topic of the teen panel can be connected to an experience, an event, or anything that the teens are interested in discussing.

Before hosting a panel in my library, I meet with students in advance to discuss the norms and expectations of the panel, the structure, and the questions. If no student is interested in moderating the panel, then I offer to moderate. The role of the moderator is to introduce the panel to the audience, ask the questions, and facilitate the discussion.

Here are some of the norms that I reinforce with the panelists in advance of the panel. Panelists should share the mic and allow all voices to have the chance to be heard, they should feel free to respond in the order in which they are seated, and they should not feel pressured to answer every question.

Here are some of the norms that I reinforce with the audience once the panel has begun. The audience should let the panelists share their ideas, they should respect the one-mic norm and not interrupt the speakers, and they should save their questions for the end because there will be an opportunity to ask the panelists questions.

Teen-Led Manga Panel Questions

A few years ago, there was a teen-led panel held in the library during Comic Con. These are the questions that engaged the panelists in a discussion about "Manga as an Acceptable Form of Reading":

1. Why do you read manga?
2. What do you learn when you read manga?
3. Why is it important for libraries to have manga in their collections?
4. Why do you think some libraries might not carry manga in their collection?
5. How might you defend reading manga to a teacher, parent, or peer?
6. How does the art style impact your understanding or appreciation of the story?
7. How does reading manga enhance your knowledge of Japanese culture?
8. What is your favorite manga series? Why?

When it comes to teen-led panels, any topic is a good topic as long as the panelists are invested in it. The librarian running the event or the panelists can create the questions, or they can be created collaboratively. The goal is to provide teens with the opportunity to practice their presentation skills, articulate their ideas, and share their voices with the community.

Promoting Manga Programs

Do not forget that promoting your library programs is just as important as creating them. Use posters, e-mails, and the library website and social media accounts to spread the word. Create print or digital sign-up sheets, event passes and tickets, and make community announcements. Visit grade-wide or departmental meetings, send personal invitations to teens and adults, and even reach out to local members of the community.

Celebrating Manga Programs

You should also showcase and celebrate the manga programs that are hosted in the library. This can be done by updating bulletin boards and display cases with pictures and projects from manga programs and events. These visual presentations will remind everyone that the library celebrates community and is a safe space for teens to explore, learn, and be themselves. These visual presentations will allow teens to showcase and celebrate their artwork, their stories, and their experiences all year round. These visual presentations will allow teens to see themselves and their journey.

TEACHING WITH MANGA

MANGA BELONGS IN CLASSROOMS NOT JUST FOR independent reading, but as an essential part of the curriculum and learning experience for students. Manga offers opportunities for students to explore literary devices and engage in literary analysis and critical thinking. The combination of images and text in manga can also provide readers with a visual representation of essential information. Readers can interpret this visual information to make connections, inferences, and build comprehension. Manga can therefore help to enrich the skills and reinforce the standards being taught in classrooms.

PROPOSING A LIBRARY ELECTIVE

At my school, twelfth-grade students are offered a variety of elective courses that they can take to receive credits towards graduation. The courses offered to students range from poetry and dance to composting and coding. But there were no electives that really connected to the pop culture themes we explore in the library, which I know many students are passionate about. So I thought it was time that I propose teaching an elective course through the library.

I was interested in teaching a manga elective course, but as a librarian, I often hear educators and parents say that they do not consider manga "real reading." Of course, I do not agree with this statement, but what really concerns me is the negative impact that it has on readers. Inspired to change their minds, I was ready to take this chance to continue to advocate for and prove that manga does in fact count as "real reading" and does belong in the classroom.

At first, I was not sure how to frame this elective course proposal to my administration, but one day an idea was born. I decided to reach out to my administration with the following proposal to teach a twelfth-grade elective course about manga.

Manga Course Proposal

In this course, students will examine how characters in manga develop their social-emotional skills. Students will read *Komi Can't Communicate*, *Beastars*, *Boys Run the Riot*, and a manga of their choice. Students will read these manga titles through the lens of CASEL's five fundamentals of social-emotional learning:

- Self-Awareness
- Self-Management
- Responsible Decision-Making
- Relationship Skills
- Social Awareness

Students will work in groups to create a reading guide for the manga of their choice. Students will present their work to the class. The reading guide will include the following elements:

- Synopsis
- Key Themes
- Key Characters
- Discussion Questions

Administrative Support

This manga course proposal was all that I sent to my administration, along with a request for a follow-up meeting. During that meeting I discussed students' investment in reading manga, the types of conversations that I have with students about manga, and why this manga course would bring value to students' educational learning experiences. To be honest, I was quite surprised when my proposal was immediately approved. The only concern that my administration had was the title of the course. They were concerned that colleges would look at a student's transcript and misunderstand a course about manga, and were afraid that colleges would assume that the course was not rigorous enough for twelfth-grade students. I was willing to compromise, so we decided on the name "Japanese Visual Storytelling" for the course. After all, that is what manga is, a form of Japanese visual storytelling. This also opened the possibility of showing anime in the course, as anime is also a form of Japanese visual storytelling. With the course approved, I could not help but share this wonderful news with every twelfth-grade student who visited the library.

Writing the Curriculum

Once the Japanese Visual Storytelling course was approved, I needed to write the curriculum for it. What made this challenging was that there was no model curriculum for teaching manga in the classroom. If manga is being taught, it is usually taught like a novel in an English class, with a focus on literary devices, literary analysis, and critical thinking. I wanted to focus on these things, as well, but I also wanted the course to be so much more. So I spent about a month writing the curriculum for the Japanese Visual Storytelling course, diving deep into my knowledge about manga and exploring all that creative energy that keeps students engaged in library programs.

Japanese Visual Storytelling Course Outline

To outline and structure the course for students so that they could anticipate their learning experiences, I created the following schedule:

- Two Weeks—Japanese Visual Storytelling
- Two Weeks—Social-Emotional Learning
- Six Weeks—Read and Discuss Manga
- Six Weeks—Manga Reading Guide Workshops and Presentations

Japanese Visual Storytelling: Lessons and Activities

The following lessons and activities follow a sequential order in the Japanese Visual Storytelling course curriculum. But each lesson and activity can also be taught as a stand-alone within a classroom or in a Manga Book Club. The course's entire curriculum does not need to be followed to bring manga into the classroom.

Manga Reading Habits (Week 1, Day 1)

During the first Japanese Visual Storytelling class we discussed the course's syllabus, the learning goals, and completed a brief Manga Reading Habits survey. I had students complete the survey so that I could get a sense of their prior knowledge and experience with manga. This data would help me to structure the lessons for students, so that all needs were being met. What excited me most about this survey data was that half the class had little or no experience with manga, and the other half of the class were manga readers with experience. Either way, they had ended up in this course together because they were interested in deepening their knowledge about manga.

As a class, we looked at the results of the Manga Reading Habits survey. I then asked the students the following questions: What surprises you about this data? What questions do you have about this data? What are the implications of these results with regard to our learning environment? What do we need to keep in mind as we move forward through this course?

Japanese Visual Storytelling Lessons (Weeks 1-2)

During the first two weeks of the course, I introduced students to the history of Japanese visual storytelling and the history of manga. The following sections include some activities from these lessons.

Activity 1: Gallery Walk

During this gallery walk, students explored multiple images that were placed around the library. I wanted students to analyze the cultural experiences reflected in a work of Japanese visual storytelling. So students had to make observations about these images and consider the following questions: What did you notice? What did you wonder about? What did you learn about Japanese visual storytelling? What did you learn about the attitudes, values, and practices of Japan?

Images from this gallery walk included:

- Picture scrolls—*Emakimono*
- Brush painting—*Sumi-e*
- Woodblock printing—*Ukiyo-e*
- Picture books—*Kusazoshi*
- Japanese theater—*Kabuki*
- Paper theater—*Kamishibai*

After the gallery walk, we got back together as a class to discuss our observations and answer the questions. I also went on to provide a lesson about these different forms of Japanese visual storytelling. Then, to supplement this learning experience, we also watched and discussed some videos about *kabuki* and *kamishibai*.

Activity 2: Manga Exploration

Since many students had never read manga, I decided it was important to provide them with a brief introduction to manga before diving into the course. I placed students in differentiated groups of four, based on their prior knowledge and experience with manga. I then gave each group a dozen manga titles. Their goal was to explore these manga titles and consider the following questions: What do you notice? What do you wonder about? What elements of Japanese visual storytelling do you see in these manga titles? What did you learn about the format, style, and content of these manga titles?

After the manga exploration, we got back together as a class to discuss our observations and answer the questions. I also went on to provide a lesson about the history of manga, the worldwide expansion of manga, and manga in the twenty-first century. Then, to supplement this learning experience, we also watched and discussed some videos about manga cafes in Japan and the *otaku* subculture.

Activity 3: Manga First Pages

During these first two weeks of the course, I also provided lessons about manga readerships, genres, age ratings, and challenges. Students also learned how to read manga, so that they could identify the correct path of the panels and text bubbles. The Manga First Pages activity provided students with the opportunity to learn and demonstrate that they could read and comprehend manga, by reading from right-to-left. During this activity, I provided students with a variety of first pages from manga series. These first pages started off simple with a few panels and text bubbles. Then they became more complex with a variety of panels and text bubbles. To be clear, there are a lot of design elements of manga that need to be shared with students so that they can have a successful reading experience. But a lot of these design elements are best taught while reading the manga, so that there is context and an investment in the learning experience. So, while students read through these first pages, they had to consider the following questions: What do you notice? What do you wonder about? What seemed familiar to you when reading the manga? What challenges did you face when reading the manga?

After students completed this activity, I assessed them individually to ensure that they could read manga correctly. Once all students had reached mastery, we were ready to move forward.

It was at this point that I let the students explore the manga collection in the library stacks, so that they could begin reading manga of their choice. I wanted students to have the chance to practice reading manga on their own before we dove into texts for the whole class. But before we would begin reading together as a class, we still had two weeks where I had to introduce students to social-emotional learning, which was the next part of the curriculum.

Social-Emotional Learning Lessons (Weeks 3–4)

During this portion of the course, students learned about social-emotional learning, CASEL's five fundamentals of SEL, the Feelings Wheel, and how to apply this knowledge to the manga they would read. The following sections provide some activities from these lessons.

Activity 1: The Five Fundamentals of Social-Emotional Learning

Learning Objective: I can define social-emotional learning and identify CASEL's five fundamentals of SEL.

- What is social-emotional learning?
- What are CASEL's five fundamentals of SEL?

After students were introduced to social-emotional learning, they read about CASEL's five fundamentals of SEL and engaged in the following protocol, adapted from CASEL's Group Reflection Protocol for SEL.[1]

This protocol allowed students to discuss the reading and comprehend the SEL framework.

1. Individually
   - Circle any word/phrase that is unclear or that you have questions about.
   - Underline any word/phrase that you connect to.

2. Small Group
   - Share out any circled words/phrases that are unclear to you or that you have questions about. Discuss what these words/phrases might mean.
   - Share out any underlined words/phrases that you connect to. Discuss why these words/phrases are significant.

3. Whole Group
   - What stands out as very important as you read and discuss SEL?
   - How does SEL connect with what you believe is important for student learning?

Activity 2: The Feelings Wheel
Learning Objective: I can use the Feelings Wheel to identify the emotions of characters within a manga.

- What is emotional intelligence?
- How do I use the Feelings Wheel to identify emotions?

After students were introduced to the Feelings Wheel, they read chapter 1 of the manga *Yuzu the Pet Vet*, vol. 1, by Mingo Ito. It was through this chapter that students were able to begin to use their knowledge of the Feelings Wheel to analyze the social-emotional development of the protagonist, Yuzu. Throughout the chapter, Yuzu learns to navigate some challenging feelings around bullying, sickness, and death. She also promises to face these challenging feelings and keep pushing herself to grow. Chapter 1 of *Yuzu the Pet Vet* was a good starting point for students to explore SEL before diving into an entire manga.

After reading chapter 1 of *Yuzu the Pet Vet*, students engaged in the following discussion:

- What life lessons did Yuzu learn?
- How did these life lessons support her social-emotional development?
- How did these life lessons support your social-emotional development?

After the success of this discussion, I knew that students were ready to begin the next part of the curriculum.

Read and Discuss Manga (Weeks 5–10)

Before students read *Komi Can't Communicate*, *Beastars*, and *Boys Run the Riot*, they read articles that gave them context for the stories and provided them with a common knowledge regarding specific topics. For example, before reading *Komi Can't Communicate*, students read and learned about social anxiety so that, when reading, they could better understand and interpret the actions of Komi, who experiences social anxiety. In another example, before reading *Boys Run the Riot*, students read and learned about the LGBTQ+ community in Japan. This way, when reading, they could understand the fears and reservations that Ryo experiences when trying to accept his trans identity. These articles helped students to better understand the social-emotional development of characters, the plot, the conflicts, and the *mangaka*'s intentions.

Manga Reading Guides

As we read the manga, we also used the manga reading guides created by Pop Culture Classroom and VIZ Media to support our learning experiences and discussions. These reading guides are free and are available for download on the Pop Culture Classroom website: popcultureclassroom.org/product-category/viz-media-reading-guides.

These manga reading guides supported me when designing the lessons and framing the warm-up questions, class discussion questions, and exit ticket questions. During the lessons, I also aligned these questions with selected pages from the manga and created slides with screenshots from the manga to prompt discussion. The students were then guided to the correct pages to find evidence, make connections, and engage in a deeper, more meaningful conversation.

What I really appreciated about the manga reading guides was that they did not just consider comprehension questions about the text. They also engaged readers in a thoughtful reflection about themselves, so that they could personally connect to the story.

Beastars Manga Reading Guide

The manga reading guide for *Beastars* is divided into different sections:

- Overview
- How to Read Manga
- Key Themes
- Key Characters
- Discussion Questions
- Activities

FIGURE 6.1 | *Beastars* Manga Reading Guide

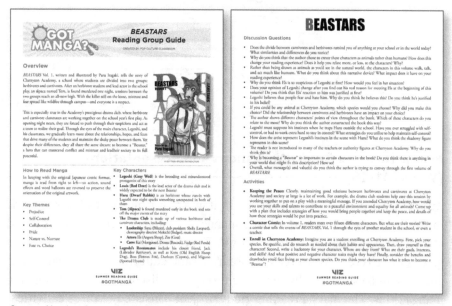

Source: Used with permission from Pop Culture Classroom

Boys Run the Riot Manga Reading Guide

The Pop Culture Classroom manga reading guides were only created to align with titles from VIZ Media. But I really wanted students to read *Boys Run the Riot*, vol. 1, by Keito Gaku, which is published by Kodansha. So, with permission from Pop Culture Classroom, I used their manga reading guide as a model to create my own manga reading guide for *Boys Run the Riot* (see figure 6.2).

FIGURE 6.2 | *Boys Run the Riot* Manga Reading Guide

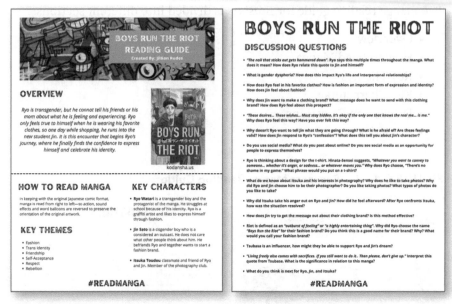

Manga Reading Guide Workshops and Presentations (Weeks 11–16)

After reading manga together as a class, it was now time for students to work in small groups of three to select a manga, read and discuss it, and create a manga reading guide of their own for it. The purpose of creating the reading guides was to create resources for librarians and educators to use that would allow them to successfully facilitate thoughtful discussions about popular manga titles. The manga reading guide project consisted of three activities: the book proposal, the manga reading guide, and the presentation. But before students dove into these projects, I provided a series of lessons.

Lesson 1: Creating High-Quality Manga Reading Guides

Students browsed the three manga reading guides that we used during this course. During this time, they had to make observations and identify what makes a high-quality manga reading guide. They considered the following questions: What key information is included in these manga reading guides? What design features make these manga reading guides high-quality? What types of questions were asked?

After this lesson, students engaged in a virtual visit with Matt Slayter, an expert from Pop Culture Classroom. Matt is the education program manager and was also the creator of the manga reading guides we used. During this visit, Matt shared with the students his process for creating the manga reading guides. He especially focused on how he created the discussion questions and he provided students with some expert tips, which included the introduction of Bloom's taxonomy. With this, he demonstrated how he formulated his questions using the taxonomy's different levels of thinking. Matt also informed students that the goal of the manga reading guides was to activate thinking and allow readers to access their background knowledge and make personal connections. He told students that they should also consider what the *mangaka* wants readers to learn from the book, and what topics and themes are consistently expressed in it. Essential to the success of a manga reading guide is how well the discussion questions invite opportunities for critical thinking and literary analysis. Students should therefore generate questions that allow readers to make inferences and draw conclusions. Matt also reminded students that the questions should be written in chronological order and should be appropriate for the age level of the readers. There was also one final piece of advice: that it would be helpful to any librarians and educators who will be facilitating the use of the manga reading guide, if it comes with any content warnings.

After we had debriefed this virtual expert visit, I reminded students to also consider incorporating some of the SEL question prompts in their reading guides (see the text box "Manga Reflection and Discussion Prompts" in chapter 4). I also provided students with a lesson about how to identify themes in manga.

Lesson 2: Identifying Themes in Manga

For the manga reading guide project, students had to identify some of the key themes represented in the manga they chose to read with their group. We defined themes as a deeper meaning or message in the manga that the reader is meant to understand.

To deepen our understanding of themes, we discussed the themes that were identified in the manga reading guides and how these themes connected to significant moments in the story.

- *Komi Can't Communicate*: communication, anxiety, friendship, courage
- *Beastars*: prejudice, self-control, pride, fate vs. choice
- *Boys Run the Riot*: trans identity, self-acceptance, respect, rebellion

To help students identify themes, I gave them the following questions to consider:

- What meaning or message about life does the *mangaka* want you to understand as a result of reading the manga?
- What are the major themes of the manga?
  - What problem is the main character facing?
  - What lesson did the main character learn?
  - What message can you take away from the story?
- How does this theme connect to the manga?

COMMON THEMES IN MANGA

- Benefits of hard work	- Importance of family
- Compassion	- Loyalty
- Courage	- Perseverance
- Death and dying	- Power of love
- Friendship	- Redemption
- Honesty	- Revenge

Activities for the Manga Reading Guides

Before the students began their manga reading guide projects, they had to consider the following questions:

1. Which manga does your group want to read?
   - Determine which manga your group will read together.
     - *Tip for selecting manga:* Each member of the reading group can research and suggest a book for the project, and then everyone can vote on which book to read.

2. What is your group's timeline?
   - Determine your schedule, what will be accomplished, and when it will be accomplished.

3. What is the format of your group's meetings?
   - Determine the format of your meetings by deciding what role each group member plays and what each group member is responsible for. Group member roles include:
     - *Group director*: Facilitates group meetings by planning the agenda, setting group goals, and taking and organizing the group notes.
     - *Question director*: Facilitates the development of the book proposal and discussion questions.
     - *Creative director*: Facilitates the creation of the manga reading guide.

4. How does your group create a reading guide?
   - Determine the format of your reading guide and decide how this will be accomplished.

Activity 1: Book Proposal

Once the students decided on their manga, they had to create a book proposal and submit it to me so that I could approve their selection. It was also essential that these titles were available through Sora, the reading app, so that I could purchase and assign a digital copy to each student in the group.

The book proposal must include the following information:

- Reading Group Members
- Manga Title
- Author/Illustrator
- Publisher
- Age Rating
- Why did your group choose this manga?
- How do you anticipate this manga connecting to CASEL's five fundamentals of social-emotional learning?

Activity 2: Manga Reading Guide

Once the book proposal was approved, students began reading and discussing the manga they had selected. Students were provided with time in class to meet with each other to set goals, read and discuss the manga, and begin work on creating the manga reading guide.

The manga reading guide had to include the following information:

- Title of Manga
- Reading Group Guide
- Created by: _____
- Book Overview
- Book Cover
- How to Read Manga
- Key Themes
- Key Characters
- Discussion Questions

Tip for creating your reading group guide: Identify significant moments in each chapter. Write down a series of questions that would allow readers to discuss these significant moments. Then, narrow down your questions to 2–3 essential questions from each chapter.

Tip for creating discussion questions: Focus on the main idea, its conflict, themes, social-emotional learning, and personal connections. Use the SEL question prompts for manga reflection (see chapter 4) to support your question development. Use any tips from our expert speaker from Pop Culture Classroom that you find useful.

Activity 3: Manga Reading Guide Presentation

After students had completed their manga reading guides, they submitted them to me for feedback. It was incredibly important that I had also read the manga that these groups chose; this way my feedback was specific not just to the format of the reading guide, but also to the quality and accuracy of the discussion questions. Once the feedback was considered and edits were made, students shared their manga reading guides with the class. Many students were inspired to read new titles just based on the presentations. (See figure 6.3, which shows an example of a student-created manga reading guide.)

After students presented their work, I asked for their permission to share their manga reading guides with Matt from Pop Culture Classroom. Students were very excited to share their work with an authentic audience.

FIGURE 6.3 | *Tokyo Ghoul* Manga Reading Guide

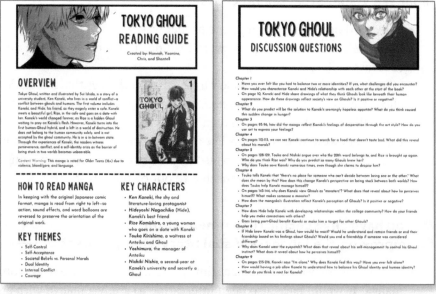

Source: Created by students in the Japanese Visual Storytelling course. Used with permission.

Japanese Visual Storytelling Evaluations

At the end of the semester, I gave students the opportunity to provide me with anonymous feedback about the Japanese Visual Storytelling course. I received the following feedback from the students; this feedback is important to review if you are considering creating your own manga course.

What are some specific things about the Japanese Visual Storytelling course or the instructor that especially helped to support student learning?

- "I liked that our instructor helped us with our projects and came around to groups to help us understand the manga."
- "There was a lot of support within the discussions after we read a specific text."
- "The instructor was a great teacher for this course since she explained everything well and all the slides and texts were clear and informative. She made sure we all were on the same page every step of the way."

What are the strengths of the Japanese Visual Storytelling course?

- "I learned how to read manga the proper way."
- "I can relate to the manga we were reading, and it really got me into the class."
- "One big strength of this course was the manga choices that Ms. Rudes chose for us. *Komi Can't Communicate*, *Beastars*, and *Boys Run the Riot* were all great choices for manga due to the variety. We discussed topics that were relevant to us like anxiety, societal beliefs/norms, and LGBTQ+ people. It was nice to also be able to choose our own manga at the end to read since it connected to our own interests."

Do you have any specific recommendations for improving the Japanese Visual Storytelling course?

- "If this course was over a longer time period, we could have read more manga! It would have also been interesting to study a manga with an anime adaptation to see how they compare."
- "Slow the pace based on the amount of time students have to read manga. Some students read manga at a slow pace."
- "I think maybe doing an independent reading assignment. Where students pick any manga, they want to read and they get to explore and go on their own journey."

A Librarian's Reflection

Overall, the Japanese Visual Storytelling course was incredibly wonderful to teach, and it thrilled me to see that students did have a valuable learning experience. I also had a lot of positive interactions with educators during and after this course. One educator would often come into the library and sit with the class, and based on our conversations together, I am pretty sure he went from completely resistant to manga to completely transformed by it. The first manga that he asked to check out and read was *Boys Run the Riot*.

Of course, at the end of the semester I also did some personal reflecting after reading the student evaluations. As a result, I identified two more activities that I plan to include in the Japanese Visual Storytelling course next time.

More Activities for the
Japanese Visual Storytelling Course ────────────────

Activity 1: Five-Minute Essays
- After reading a manga, students will be provided with a quiet space to think
- Students will use question prompts that inspire a critical voice
- Students will write for five minutes and then share their ideas with the class

Activity 2: Character Infographic (w/ Canva)
- Students will select one character from a manga that they read in class
- Students will identify the social and emotional strengths of the character
- Students will use this information to create an infographic of the character

Additional goals that I am setting for next year include reading more manga, watching more anime, hosting Socratic seminars, finding opportunities for creative activities, creating a collaboration tracker for the project, and more.

NOTE

1. "Group Reflection Protocol for SEL," CASEL, 2020, https://casel.s3.us-east-2.amazonaws.com/CASEL-Wheel-SEL-Reflection.pdf.

CONCLUSION
Manga Sparks Joy

Joy is an emotional response to something that brings you pleasure, makes you happy, brightens your day, gets you excited, satisfies you, and fulfills you. For many, reading manga sparks joy.

As a librarian, I do not just passively put books on the shelves, hope they get checked out, and assume students have positive reading experiences. I want to ensure that I am actively building a reflective and rewarding culture in the library.

With that, I decided to sit down with some seventh-grade students to ask them questions about their manga reading experiences. In this casual conversation, I asked students a few questions to see if manga did in fact spark joy.

How do you feel when you read manga?

- "When I read manga, it makes me feel an emotional range of 'Wow!' and 'Damn!'"
- "It gets me energized and I want to read more."
- "It gets you hooked and you want to keep reading."
- "Manga makes me feel better than regular books."
- "It's fun!"
- "Intrigued. What is going to happen?!"
- "Excited! I want to go home and read and do nothing else!"
- "I get emotionally invested."
- "When I read I get lost in my own world."
- "Relax and chill."
- "Stay up late to read."
- "I get into a zone and the world around me disappears."

- "Happy and calm."
- "Good experience."
- "Takes away distractions."
- "I don't have to read for school. I do it for myself."
- "I can read manga every day."

What do you like most about reading manga?

- "Sometimes I just find myself staring at the art."
- "Good storylines motivate me to read."
- "I become the character. I am the character."
- "Manga lasts a long time so you can invest."
- "The art is realistic and visually stunning."
- "I am always thinking about it because it engages me. Regular books are boring."
- "I picture the manga moving and I add color."
- "Engaged in what is happening."
- "I feel like I have a relationship with the characters. I can relate. I feel an emotional bond."
- "I like to read about their backstory and their family."
- "Can't wait to see what happens."
- "I like to try new things. New series. New genres."
- "Manga is such a mix of emotions."
- "I like to witness their life."
- "I'm interested in watching the characters grow up."
- "New opportunities to think about life."
- "It's a gateway to reading."
- "I can use my imagination and picture myself being there."
- "There is something to read for everyone's enjoyment."

What do you learn when reading manga?

- "Learn about friends. What a friend is doing wrong, see red flags."
- "The way you respond to things emotionally matters."
- "I learned about trust. Be careful who you trust."
- "Never back down. Push yourself to your limits."
- "Determination."

- "I learn how to act, how to be social, and how to have relationships."
- "I learn Japanese, I learn about other places, what they eat. . ."
- "People can change."
- "Different perspectives. Understand others."
- "Character development is life changing."
- "Accomplish something new."
- "I learn about trust and honesty."
- "Cherish the moments you have."
- "See the perspective of your friends so you can help."
- "Life lessons in manga can help you in your own life."

■   ■   ■

The students' responses completely surprised me—not because they had positive reading experiences with manga, but because they were able to articulate those experiences in a way that was crucial to their social-emotional development. To see that students were so thoughtfully reflective in their engagement with manga was truly impressive and inspiring.

Building the manga collection and the library culture can take some effort but it is worth it because manga can empower readers, transform lives, and spark joy.

APPENDIX A
Manga in Libraries Webinars

The Manga in Libraries webinars were presented by a diverse and interdisciplinary group of experts from the field. These experts include, but are not limited to, librarians, educators, podcasters, journalists, and publishers. To continue your manga professional development, check out the Manga in Libraries webinars. Each webinar also includes a book list and resource list that were collaboratively created by the webinar panelists. The webinars, book lists, and resource lists can also be found at MangaInLibraries.com.

WEBINAR #1: WHY MANGA?

In this webinar, experts discuss the importance of including manga in the collection, suggestions for purchasing them, resources for collection development, and more.

Discussion Questions

- Why is it important that we have manga in our libraries? Why should librarians invest in manga? What value does manga have for our readers?
- What is the most popular manga series in your library?
- What "must have" manga should be on all library shelves?
- How much shelving in your library is dedicated to the manga section? How do you organize the manga? Do you have any special features in the manga section?
- How do you deal with the wear and tear of manga?
- What resources do you use for collection development?

View the webinar on YouTube: bit.ly/MILwebinar1
View the book list on Anime Planet: bit.ly/MILbook1
View the resource list on Google Docs: bit.ly/MILresource1

WEBINAR #2: REPRESENTATION OF GIRLS AND WOMEN

In this webinar, experts discuss the social context of gender expectations in Japan, sexuality and fan service in manga, titles with positive representation, and more.

Discussion Questions

- What are the cultural expectations of girls and women in Japan (traditional and modern)? What do we need to understand about gender expectations in Japan? How might this knowledge influence our understanding of the manga that we read?
- When it comes to gender, sexuality, and identity, how is manga used as an expressive outlet for *mangaka*?
- What is fan service? What elements of fan service could be considered problematic?
- How are girls typically represented in *shojo*? What stereotypes might this perpetuate?
- What manga titles can you recommend that have positive representations of girls and women? Are there any particular *mangaka* that we should consider?

View the webinar on YouTube: bit.ly/MILwebinar2
View the book list on Anime Planet: bit.ly/MILbook2
View the resource list on Google Docs: bit.ly/MILresource2

WEBINAR #3: MANGA AND ANIME PROGRAMMING

In this webinar, experts discuss building a library culture, hosting manga and anime programming, popular manga and anime series, and more.

Discussion Questions

- Why is it important to build this type of culture in the library? How does manga and anime programming foster this culture?
- Can you tell us about a manga or anime event or a club that you host in your library?
- How do you decide what anime to watch or what manga to read? How do you decide if it's a "best fit" for the audience?
- While watching anime and reading manga, what are some of the things that you discuss with the youth?
- Have you faced any challenges because of your manga and anime clubs? Has there been resistance from the community? Or is your programming fully supported?
- What has been a popular manga or anime in your library? Why?

View the webinar on YouTube: bit.ly/MILwebinar3
View the book list on Anime Planet: bit.ly/MILbook3
View the resource list on Google Docs: bit.ly/MILresource3

WEBINAR #4: DEFENDING THE COLLECTION

In this webinar, experts discuss manga challenges and censorship, tips for collection development, titles worth defending, and more.

Discussion Questions

- How do you justify purchasing manga? Why should readers have access to manga?
- What are the most common reasons for manga challenges? What are some common misconceptions about manga?
- Have you ever dealt with (or know of) a manga challenge? If so, what was the challenge and what was the process?
- What is the difference between censorship and collection development? Do you have a collection development policy for manga (or tips/suggestions of things to include in a policy)?
- Do you use publisher ratings to help with collection development? How do you decide what is appropriate and what is not for the intended audience?
- What are some titles worth defending?

View the webinar on YouTube: bit.ly/MILwebinar4
View the book list on Anime Planet: bit.ly/MILbook4
View the resource list on Google Docs: bit.ly/MILresource4

WEBINAR #5: SUPPORTING ALL LEARNERS

In this webinar, experts discuss the literary value of manga, supporting the needs of all learners, titles for book clubs, and more.

Discussion Questions

- What is the literary value of manga? What skills and strengths can readers develop?
- Do you have any experience working with a specific group of learners, and if so, can you tell us about this group and how reading manga supports their learning needs?
- Have you ever taught manga in the classroom or hosted a manga book club? If so, what did you read and why? If not, what manga would you read and why?
- Have you received any feedback from students or from other librarians, educators, and administrators about the value of manga . . . especially from those who maybe did not initially consider manga as "real reading"?
- Do you know any resources that could help with teaching manga in the classroom or hosting a manga book club?

View the webinar on YouTube: bit.ly/MILwebinar5
View the book list on Anime Planet: bit.ly/MILbook5
View the resource list on Google Docs: bit.ly/MILresource5

WEBINAR #6: SPOOKY AND SCARY MANGA

In this webinar, experts discuss spooky and scary myths and legends in manga, why readers like to be scared, titles for collection development, and more.

Discussion Questions

- What is your favorite spooky and scary myth or legend in manga?
- Professor Rogals, what can you tell us about the role of the supernatural in Japanese culture?
- Why do spooky and scary stories appeal to readers? Why does spooky and scary manga offer a lot of crossover appeal to non-manga readers? What makes spooky and scary manga a unique media format?
- Julia and Masumi, what is your professional relationship to spooky and scary manga?
- How do we know what is age appropriate for readers? How do we know if manga is too spooky and scary for readers?
- Do you have any recommendations for spooky and scary manga?

View the webinar on YouTube: bit.ly/MILwebinar6
View the book list on Anime Planet: bit.ly/MILbook6
View the resource list on Google Docs: bit.ly/MILresource6

WEBINAR #7: THE LGBTQ+ COMMUNITY

In this webinar, experts discuss the LGBTQ+ community in Japan, creating safe spaces and programs, titles for collection development, and more.

Discussion Questions

- How do you support or how could you support the LGBTQ+ community in your library?
- Erica, you are the founder of Yuricon. Could you tell us about this event and how it supports members of the LGBTQ+ community?
- What do we know about the LGBTQ+ community in Japan and the representation of LGBTQ+ characters in manga?
- TJ and Ivan, what is your professional relationship to LGBTQ+ manga?
- We often find that LGBTQ+ manga titles are given the age rating of 16+. Why do publishers give this rating? Why might this be problematic for readers and librarians?
- Do you have any recommendations for LGBTQ+ manga?

View the webinar on YouTube: bit.ly/MILwebinar7
View the book list on Anime Planet: bit.ly/MILbook7
View the resource list on Google Docs: bit.ly/MILresource7

WEBINAR #8: SOCIAL-EMOTIONAL LEARNING

In this webinar, experts discuss how manga can support the social-emotional development of teens, finding community, titles for collection development, and more.

Discussion Questions

- How can manga also be a support system for the social-emotional development of teens?
- Tiffany, can you give us a better understanding of CASEL and how it relates to teens and manga?
- It is not just the manga itself that teens are drawn to, so what other aspects of this fandom engages teens?
- Mark, what is your professional relationship to manga?
- Renee and Joe, you presented on the panel "Teen Talk through Manga" and at both New York Comic Con and Anime NYC. Can you tell us a little bit about this panel and how it connects manga to the social-emotional learning of teens?
- Do you have any recommendations for manga that supports the social-emotional development of teens?

View the webinar on YouTube: bit.ly/MILwebinar8
View the book list on Anime Planet: bit.ly/MILbook8
View the resource list on Google Docs: bit.ly/MILresource8

WEBINAR #9: MANGA 101

In this webinar, experts discuss the history of manga, its readership and genres, translation and localization, age ratings and resources, supply chain "issues," manga recommendations, and more.

Discussion Questions

- Deb, what can you tell us about the history and cultural context of manga?
- Ivan, what are the differences between manga and U.S. and Canadian comics?
- Zack, what's the process for translating and localizing a manga into English?
- Laura, what can you tell us about manga readerships and genres?
- Jillian, can you help us to understand the age ratings publishers use and provide us with some resources to support collection development?
- Ben, what can you tell us about the supply chain "issues"?

View the webinar on YouTube: bit.ly/MIlwebinar9
View the book list on Anime Planet: bit.ly/MILbook9
View the resource list on Google Docs: bit.ly/MILresource9

WEBINAR #10: BIPOC REPRESENTATION

In this webinar, experts discuss the importance of BIPOC representation in manga, BIPOC artists/authors, celebrating identity in libraries, book recommendations, and more.

Discussion Questions

- What has been your personal relationship with representation in manga? Why is it important that readers see themselves and their stories represented in manga?
- How do you sit within your own identity pocket in light of what is pushed as "popular" or "marketable" in the industry?
- It's important that representation be a spectrum, so that we avoid creating new stereotypes or playing deeply into respectability politics. What are your thoughts on inclusivity and the villains we love, even if we hate them?
- Do you think BIPOC representation should increase in manga? Do you think BIPOC artists/authors can break into the forefront of the manga industry? If so, why and how?

- How can librarians support a sense of belonging and celebrate identity in their libraries?
- What manga titles do you suggest that have positive representations of BIPOC characters? What resources do you suggest for librarians to use for identifying these titles for collection development?

View the webinar on YouTube: bit.ly/MILwebinar10
View the book list on Anime Planet: bit.ly/MILbook10
View the resource list on Google Docs: bit.ly/MILresource10

WEBINAR #11: TEACHING WITH MANGA

In this webinar, experts discuss the benefits of including manga in the curriculum, manga titles and lessons, addressing challenges, resources for teaching support, and more.

Discussion Questions

- Why do you think manga has yet to make it into the "mainstream," the "standard" curriculum? Is it because of misconceptions, challenges, lack of access, and so on?
- How can educators and librarians use manga to support the literacy skills of readers?
- How can educators and librarians use manga to support readers' social-emotional development?
- Have you ever taught a manga class or hosted a manga book club? If so, what was your approach? What manga/lessons did you teach? Or how might the content and the resources that you have created support the teaching of manga?
- Do you have any titles to suggest for teaching with manga? What themes or standards might these titles connect to?

View the webinar on YouTube: bit.ly/MILwebinar11
View the book list on Anime Planet: bit.ly/MILbook11
View the resource list on Google Docs: bit.ly/MILresource11

WEBINAR #12: DISABILITY VISIBILITY IN MANGA

In this webinar, experts discuss the importance of disability representation in manga, resources for supporting all patrons, manga titles with disability visibility, and more.

Discussion Questions

- Why does representation matter in our libraries, our collections, and our programs?
- How can libraries and librarians support patrons with disabilities? What services and resources could we provide that would support access to manga?
- How has the portrayal of disabilities evolved in manga? Why is it important that manga has realistic representations of characters with disabilities?
- Have you seen your own lived experiences reflected in manga? If so, what manga? If not, what would you like to see?
- What would you like librarians who are selecting manga with disability visibility to know?
- What manga titles do you suggest that have positive representations of characters with disabilities? What resources do you suggest for librarians to use for identifying these titles for collection development?

Watch the webinar on YouTube: bit.ly/MILwebinar12
View the book list on Anime Planet: bit.ly/MILbook12
View the resource list on Google Docs: bit.ly/MILresource12

APPENDIX B
Manga Book Lists

CHAPTER 1: Manga 101

Adachi and Shimamura

Ascendance of a Bookworm

Attack on Titan

Berserk

Bleach

Bloom into You

Boys Run the Riot

Bungo Stray Dogs

Cardcaptor Sakura

Chi's Sweet Home

Creepy Cat

Death Note

Erased

Given

Golden Kamuy

Horimiya

I Want to Be a Wall

I'm in Love with the Villainess

Jujutsu Kaisen

Kaiju Girl Caramelise

Kaiju No. 8

Knights of Sidonia

Laid Back Camp

Little Witch Academia

Mobile Suit Gundam

Monthly Girls' Nozaki-kun

My Hero Academia

My Love Mix-Up!

Naruto

Neon Genesis Evangelion

Nicola Traveling Around the
  Demons' World

One Piece

Our Dining Table

Our Dreams at Dusk

Perfect World

Pokémon Adventures

Princess Jellyfish

Sailor Moon

Sasaki and Miyano

So I'm a Spider, So What?

Sweetness & Lightning

Tokyo Ghoul

Ultraman

The Way of the Househusband

Whisper Me a Love Song

Witch Hat Atelier

Wotakoi: Love Is Hard for Otaku

Yo-kai Watch

CHAPTER 2: Manga Collection Development

Asadora!

Ascendance of a Bookworm

Attack on Titan

Beauty and the Beast of Paradise
   Lost

Bleach

Blue Lock

Blue Period

Cardcaptor Sakura

Cat Massage Therapy

Chi's Sweet Home

Creepy Cat

Death Note

Demon Slayer

Dr. Stone

The Elusive Samurai

Erased

The Evil Secret Society of Cats

The Fox and Little Tanuki

Fruits Basket

Fullmetal Alchemist

The Girl from the Other Side

Haikyu!!

Horimiya

Jujutsu Kaisen

Kaguya-sama: Love Is War

Kaiju No. 8

Little Witch Academia

Look Back

Lovely Muco!

My Hero Academia

My Love Story!

My Love Mix-Up!

My Neighbor Seki

My Neighbor Totoro

Naruto

Nicola Traveling Around the
   Demons' World

One Piece

One-Punch Man

Ouran High School Host Club

Perfect World

Penguin & House

Pokémon Adventures

A Polar Bear in Love

The Promised Neverland

Ranma 1/2

Rooster Fighter

Sailor Moon

A Sign of Affection

A Silent Voice

Splatoon

Spy x Family

Toilet-Bound Hanako-kun

Tokyo Ghoul

A Tropical Fish Yearns for Snow

Wandance

The Way of the Househusband

Witch Hat Atelier

Yokai Watch

Yotsuba&!

your name.

CHAPTER 3: Representation in Manga

Apple Black

Attack on Titan

Beastars

Bleach

Cardcaptor Sakura

Carole & Tuesday

Clock Striker

Doughnuts under a Crescent Moon

Dragonball

Even Though We're Adults

Fire Force

Fruits Basket

Haikyu!!

Hammer

How Do We Relationship

Hunter x Hunter

I Hear the Sunspot

I'm in Love with the Villainess

Kimi Ni Todoke

Komi Can't Communicate

March Comes in like a Lion

My Brain Is Different: Stories of
    ADHD and Other Developmental

Disorders

My Hero Academia

My Wandering Warrior Existence

One Piece

Overlord

Perfect World

The Promised Neverland

QQ Sweeper

Queen's Quality

Real

The Rose of Versailles

Saigami

Sailor Moon

Satoko & Nada

Sex Education 120%

Shino Can't Say Her Name

A Sign of Affection

Skip Beat!

Slam Dunk

Snow White with the Red Hair

Soul Eater

Still Sick

Sweat and Soap

CHAPTER 4: Social-Emotional Learning and Manga

Beastars

Boys Run the Riot

Demon Slayer

The Golden Sheep

Haikyu!!

I Think Our Son Is Gay

I Want to Be a Wall

Komi Can't Communicate

Love in Focus

Our Dreams at Dusk

Perfect World

The Promised Neverland

A Silent Voice

Wandance

Yuzu the Pet Vet

CHAPTER 6: Teaching with Manga

Beastars
Boys Run the Riot
Komi Can't Communicate
Tokyo Ghoul
Yuzu the Pet Vet

INDEX

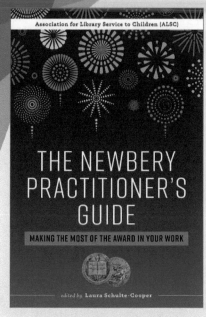